Focus On 3D Models

Evan Pipho

PREMIER PRESS

GAME DEVELOPMENT

Premier

Press

Publisher: Stacy L. Hiquet

Marketing Manager: Heather Hurley

Acquisitions Editor: Mitzi Foster Koontz

Project/Copy Editor: Kezia Endsley

Technical Reviewer: Kelly Dempski

Interior Layout: Danielle Foster

Cover Designer: Mike Tanamachi

Indexer: Kelly Talbot

Proofreader: Jenny Davidson

Wolfenstein, Doom, and Quake are copyrights of id Software. Half-Life is a copyright of VALVe Software. Unreal is a copyright of Epic MegaGames. The Descent series of games are copyrights of Parallax. MilkShape 3D was created by the chUmbaLum sOft company.

Discreet is a division of Autodesk, Inc., 3d Studio Max, 3D Studio VIZ, Character Studio, Fire, Flame, Flint, Frost, Inferno, Lightscape, Smoke, Stream, and Wire are registered trademarks, and Discreet, 3ds Max, Backdraft, Combustion, Jobnet, and Sparks are trademarks of Autodesk, Inc., Discreet Logic Inc. in the USA and/or other countries. Mental ray is a registered trademark of mental images GmbH & Co. KG. Vecta3D-MAX is a trademark of IdeaWorks3D, Ltd. All other brand names, product names, or trademarks belong to their respective holders. (c) Copyright 2002 Autodesk, Inc. All rights reserved.

Important: Premier Press cannot provide software support. Please contact the appropriate software manufacturer's technical support line or Web site for assistance.

Premier Press and the author have attempted throughout this book to distinguish proprietary trademarks from descriptive terms by following the capitalization style used by the manufacturer.

Information contained in this book has been obtained by Premier Press from sources believed to be reliable. However, because of the possibility of human or mechanical error by our sources, Premier Press, or others, the Publisher does not guarantee the accuracy, adequacy, or completeness of any information and is not responsible for any errors or omissions or the results obtained from use of such information. Readers should be particularly aware of the fact that the Internet is an ever-changing entity. Some facts may have changed since this book went to press.

ISBN: 1-59200-033-9
Library of Congress Catalog Card Number: 2002111229
Printed in the United States of America
03 04 05 06 07 BH 10 9 8 7 6 5 4 3 2 1

Premier Press, a division of Course Technology
2645 Erie Avenue, Suite 41
Cincinnati, Ohio 45208

Acknowledgments

First off, thanks to my parents for letting me do this; without their support and putting up with not seeing me most of the summer this would have never been possible.

A big thanks to Trent Polack for helping me secure this book deal and for being an awesome friend and programmer. Without you I would have never made it to where I am today.

I can't forget all of the great people over at gamedev.net, flipcode.com, and their associated chat rooms. You guys have been invaluable in helping me sort through problems, squash bugs, and are just great friends. There are too many to name, but a few who have proved to be invaluable have been Nicholas Cooper, Sean Kent, Denis Lukianov, Ron Penton, and Henrik Stuart.

To my friend and lifesaver Amy for forcefully dragging me away from my computer and out of my room every so often; it kept me from going insane.

Thanks to all of my other friends who put up with not seeing me much at all during the summer.

Last, but definitely not least, a huge thanks to the people over at Premier Press, especially Mitzi for sticking with me the whole time I was writing. Your support has been terrific, even through computer, Internet, and communications problems. All of the editors who worked on this have been great; all of you have taught me many valuable lessons as I have worked on my first book. I hope to work with all of you again.

About the Author

Evan Pipho has always been interested in computers and electronics. As a young child, he learned to operate his dad's IBM PC, playing games, and experimenting with the many programs it contained. While playing with his dad's Windows machine, he started to look at languages such as QBASIC and C and to pursue his life-long interest in game development. He had decided a long time ago that he wanted to pursue game development, so he dug right in. After some classes at the nearby community college and several maddening months in front of the computer, he was hooked!

You can visit the author's forums at http://www.codershq.com. Click the Forums link. If you prefer private email to public forums, you can contact him at evan@codershq.com.

Contents at a Glance

Contents

CHAPTER 7   THE 3DS MODELS 109

CHAPTER 8   MDL, THE LEGENDARY HALF-LIFE FORMAT 127

CHAPTER 9   ENTER THE QUAKE! QUAKE III's MD3 FORMAT 135

CHAPTER 10   TIPS, TRICKS, AND METHODS 153

APPENDIX A   COMMON 3D MODEL FORMATS 165

APPENDIX B   STL VECTOR PRIMER 169

APPENDIX C   GOING ABOVE AND BEYOND 183

LETTER FROM THE SERIES EDITOR

As a 3D game programmer, sooner or later the time comes when you get bored with spinning cubes and flying space ships in space. You want fully articulated 3D characters and animation. So you start looking on Internet for information thereof, and sooner or later you realize that although there are a lot of sites with information—and lots of demos—it's all rather useless in reality. There are too many holes in the file format explanations, and in the end you would probably be better off reverse-engineering the files rather than wade through hacker document after hacker document.

This problem is one that I have personally been dealing with for a long time. When I first wanted to write a Quake file loader, I thought that it would be easy; there must be a billion sites on the Internet with clear and concise explanations, right? However, there is none! As far as I can tell there is literally only one single document on the Internet with the .MD2 file format, and it's not complete, but more of a FAQ. Moreover, it's just a file format; it doesn't really explain all the details. This is just one example. There are many. The bottom line is that whether it's a game format like Quake's .MD2 or .MD3 or 3D Studio Max's file format, there is simply no single place to find information. This issue was the motivation for this book.

My goal for this book was to give you a single reference for the most popular file formats, but at the same time teach you how to use them. That is, it's useless to show how to read each key frame from a .MD2 file if you don't know how to interpolate them. Thus, the author, Evan Pipho, has not only covered every important file format (within reason), but he has also covered foundational material such as mathematics, skeletal animation, and more. If you open this book not knowing a single thing about 3D character animation, by the end of the book you will know how to work with all the popular file formats, how to write readers, and how to actually animate the meshes in real-time in your applications. Of course, this book assumes that you are familiar with 3D graphics, DirectX (or OpenGL) and you can create a rudimentary 3D engine either leveraging an API or manually with software that at minimum can render polygons and perform clipping, projection, and rasterization.

Nevertheless, I can't tell you how excited I am about this book. It's the first of its kind—there is not a single other book on the market that illustrates all these file formats from a game programmer's point of view.

In conclusion, this is yet another book that no 3D game programmer can do without. As I write this letter the book isn't even printed yet, but I am printing out a hard copy just to have it on my desk to refer to!

Sincerely,

Andre' LaMothe

Series Editor for Premier Press's *Game Development* Series

Introduction and Overview

A new trend is creeping into video games at an incredible rate. This trend makes games more realistic, more believable, and in some cases, more fun. A large percentage of new games use this trend, and consumers are gobbling these games up as fast as they can be made. This new trend, of course, is the use of 3D. From the player models to the virtual game worlds, players are demanding some form of 3D interaction. This idea of 3D interaction encompasses many genres, even those that have traditionally been 2D. Games such as *Blizzard's Warcraft 3* have brought 3D interaction into the "Real Time Strategy" genre, a genre generally dominated by 2D games. Even puzzle and other "value games" are starting to hook into the idea of 3D.

At the same time, hardware manufacturers are creating better and faster hardware. Ultra-fast processors and graphics cards capable of handling millions of pieces of 3D geometry every second are becoming very commonplace in the average home computer. This allows you as a game developer to write more realistic and graphically intensive games without causing the average consumers' computers to crawl under a rock at the sight of them. New generations of graphics cards are allowing more and more of the calculations to be done on the graphics card, freeing up the processor to concentrate on other aspects of the game, such as sound, enemy AI, and, well, even more graphical effects.

Many companies have realized that 3D is the future of video games and have worked to provide players with top-rate graphics and realism, including the following:

- id Software (http://www.idsoftware.com) Starting in 1992, the creators of the revolutionary Wolfenstein, Doom, and Quake series were one of the first companies to realize the 3D dream. Their 3D engines have been licensed by other companies for use in countless games.

- VALVe Software (http://www.valvesoftware.com) Even though VALVe came in a little later than id, it still rocked the world with the release of Half-Life in November of 1998. The graphical aspect of Half-Life was mind-boggling, not to mention the

id Software's Quake III

advanced AI and the superb story line. For the first time, advanced technologies such as skeletal animation and colored lighting were available on the home computer.

- *Epic MegaGames* (http://www.epicgames.com)   With its beautiful Unreal Engine, Epic opened the world for games with large outside areas, putting an end to the claustrophobic corridors and tiny rooms of earlier games.

- Parallax (http://www.pxsoftware.com/)   Parallax showed gamers how wondrous a full six degrees of freedom could be. With its Descent series of games, Parallax opened the doors to a whole new dimension in the 3D game industry.

- 3DFX   I can't overlook the contributions of the now deceased video chipset manufacturer. 3DFX introduced the general public to the miracle of 3D hardware 3D acceleration with the release of the Voodoo series of video cards. They were the fastest you could buy until nVidia released their TnT2 Ultra. The capability of the home PC to accelerate 3D graphics paved the way for new, graphically advanced games.

VALVe's groundbreaking Half-Life

The incredible Unreal Engine in Epic's Unreal

These companies and games are but a few of the many contributors to the 3D phenomenon. Many games have come and gone, unnoticed by the general public, and even to most gamers. Even so, a few of them have introduced new technologies and ideas that have changed the face of the gaming world forever.

Goals for This Book

Chances are if you are reading this, you either just got the book, or you are standing in a bookstore trying to decide whether you should get it. If you are interested in creating 3D games, this book shows you how to implement one to work with one of the most important parts, 3D models. Open up one of your favorite 3D game, preferably a first person shooter type. Look around you; see those enemies over there? Or how about that health pack and weapon sitting in the corner waiting for you to pick up? All of these features are created by 3D models created by the artists and loaded into the game by programmers like you.

So now you are probably wondering, "how will I benefit if I get this book and what will I learn?" You will learn all sorts of cool stuff here. After you read this you should be able to:

- Understand how to load various 3D model formats.
- Display and animate various types of models in your programs.
- Understand how *skeletal animation*, the innovation that uses "bones" within models for animation purposes, works. *Skeletal animation* uses "bones" and "joints" attached to the model's mesh to perform animation. Skeletal animation has many advantages over traditional keyframe animation, including reduced storage space, increased ease of animation for the artists, and more realistic motion. You will learn much more about this amazing technology later in the book.
- Attach models to other models to form more complex objects.

The first two chapters are dedicated to a review of important math skills, with a quick review of vectors and matrices. Then, after you read the review of the elusive quaternion, you should be set for most of the math used in the remaining chapters.

After reviewing the necessary math skills, you move right into some of the less complicated formats such as OBJ (Chapter 4) and MD2 (Chapter 5). You will walk through the data structures and loading procedures needed for each type. Code is sprinkled through the text in the form of small functions or data structures, but there are never any large code dumps.

From these simple formats, you will go on to learn about two of the most important and useful technologies in 3D models: skeletal animation and tagging. You already learned what skeletal animation is in the previous bulleted list.

Tagging, as many call it, is the capability to attach models so that they move together. This technique is used to do things such as attach weapon models to the hands of characters, or even piece models together from parts, such as a head, torso, and leg models. Read on to Chapter 9 and you will learn more about this useful technology, and how it applies to Quake 3's MD3 format.

After you learn about the needed math and play a bit with the simple formats, , you can take a look at loading some of the more complicated formats. Some of these will be skeletally animated using the techniques described in the previous chapters, and some contain tags to make up a full character model. Again, every detail of the formats will be outlined to allow easy implementation in your own game.

Who Should Read This Book

You do not need a lot of programming experience to use this book. All of the code shown throughout the book is written in C++, so a basic understanding of C/C++ is a must. The demos on the CD are written using C++, with OpenGL as the graphics API. I tried to keep all of the code and demos as simple as possible to make porting to other languages and graphics APIs possible. Because of this, the demos may not be optimized as much as they could be, so feel free to look for ways to optimize and speed them up.

If you need to brush up on either C++ or OpenGL, I recommend you visit http://www.gametutorials.com and http://nehe.gamedev.net for help. Other good references include books from the Premier Game Programming series. *OpenGL Game Programming* and *Game Programming All*

In One will put you in an excellent position for the rest of the book. Once you have a decent grasp of C++ and OpenGL, you are almost ready to begin your journey into the wide world of 3D.

This book assumes you can create a rudimentary 3D engine, either by leveraging an API or manually with software that, at minimum, can render polygons and perform clipping, projection, and rasterization.

You will also need to have a good understanding of algebra and trigonometry. Understanding vectors, matrices, and quaternions is also important. If you feel uncomfortable with any of those (except maybe the quaternion part; no one really ever feels comfortable with them), I would suggest a quick visit to http://www.math.com for algebra and trigonometry, and a review Chapters 1 and 2 for a review of vector, matrix, and quaternion math.

Now you are ready to conquer 3D models. Have fun!

What's on the CD

As you have probably noticed, there is a CD attached to the back cover of the book. There is lots of cool stuff on there. All of the source code for all the model formats discussed in the book, plus a few extras for formats that just didn't fit are included. Also included are extra 3D models made by the game development community. Please check the README file for each of the models before using them in your own projects. The README files contain each author's name, email address, and any terms of use that he or she has put forth regarding the use of his or her artwork.

Digging deeper on the CD, you will find various tools used in manufacturing 3D models and other related objects, such as skins and textures. Also included are shareware and trial versions of popular software. Try them all and see which ones you want to purchase and keep.

An extras folder contains various projects and source code written by other members of the community. As with the artwork, please read the README files included with everything to avoid any copyright infringement.

Occasionally there will be bug fixes and updates for the source code on the CD. Check out http://books.codershq.com. I hope in the future to release more loaders for other types of 3D models, as well as port them to other languages and APIs, so check the site often.

A Final Word Before You Start

I hope you find this book useful as you start writing your dream 3D game. The best thing to do is try to write your own code from the text, instead of copying it from the examples. You will learn much more that way. If you are frustrated at first, just keep trying; it will come to you. Even the big names in the 3D game industry didn't get it right the first time. Remember, the most important element of game development is to *have fun*! Enjoy the book.

CHAPTER I

REVIEWING MATRICES AND VECTORS

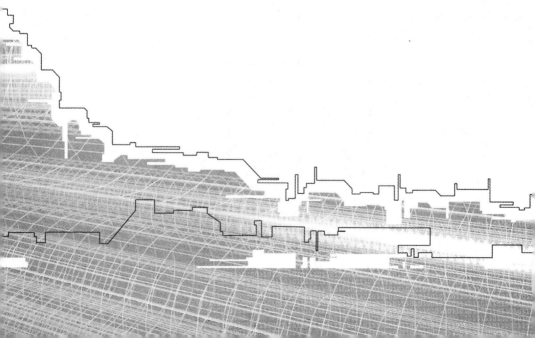

A s you surf the Internet, learning how to make the next big 3D game, you inevitably come across references to "matrices" and "vectors". If you have not had the pleasure of taking any math courses beyond high school, you may have little or no experience with either subject. This chapter takes you through the basic matrix and vector operations you need to create your own game, as well as provides full source code to a set of matrix and vector classes. This chapter provides you with enough information to help you in your adventure into 3D graphics. Although vector and matrix operations are discussed, the theory behind them is not discussed in depth. There is a great site available on the Web if you want to go more in-depth called *Mathworld*. Check out Eric Weisstein's *World of Mathematics*, available at `http://mathworld.wolfram.com`.

Understanding and Using Matrices

Just what is a matrix you ask? Well, simply put, a matrix is a rectangular array of numbers. A few examples of matrices are shown in Figure 1.1. You know what they look like, but just what are they good for? Well, mathematicians like to use them to represent systems of linear equations. Using matrix operations, it is possible to solve these systems with much less work than using other methods, such as substitution, to solve them. In computer graphics, however, matrices are used to represent *transformations*. Transformations are essentially rotations and translation values for an object. The nice thing about using matrices for this type of thing is the fact that transformations can be combined using simple algebra, making it easy for you, and fast within your programs.

Most of the matrices that are used in graphics programming are square matrices. A square matrix is simply a matrix that has the same number of rows as columns. The leftmost matrix in Figure 1.1 is a square matrix. Generally, 3D math only requires matrices that are 3×3 or 4×4 elements. For clarity, and to simply keep the size of the figures

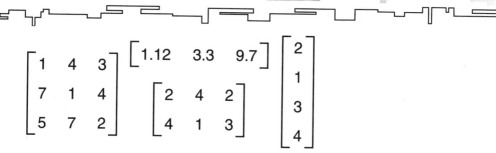

Figure 1.1 *A few examples of matrices. Notice that they can be square or rectangular; two dimensions or one.*

down, all the matrices in this chapter from now on will be 3×3 square matrices. Keep in mind that the same principles that apply to 3×3 matrices will also work on 4×4 matrices.

As you work with OpenGL, D3D, or any other graphics API, you will notice that they use mostly 4×4 matrices. There is a very good reason for this. A 4×4 matrix is capable of not only storing rotation values, but they can also store the *translation,* or movement values, at the same time. This eliminates the need to keep track of two separate sets of values for rotation and translation.

Individual elements of a matrix are denoted by the notation a_{ij}. The a is standard notation, the i is the number of the row the element resides in, and the j is the number of the column. Therefore, a matrix could be written as shown in Figure 1.2.

$$\begin{bmatrix} a_{11} & a_{12} & a_{13} \\ a_{21} & a_{22} & a_{23} \\ a_{31} & a_{32} & a_{33} \end{bmatrix}$$

Figure 1.2 *A 3×3 matrix drawn using matrix notation. Note that the first subscript represents the row and the second subscript represents the column of the element.*

The Zero and the Identity Matrices

If you recall your elementary school math experience, you hopefully remember that anything plus zero doesn't change the original number, nor does anything multiplied by one. Well, the same thing is true for matrices. For addition and subtraction of matrices you use what is known as the *zero matrix*. Adding or subtracting a zero matrix to or from any other matrix will result in a matrix identical to the original, just like adding zero to a real number gives you your original number. A zero matrix is exactly what it sounds like, a matrix full of zeros. Every element in the zero matrix contains a value of zero. A 3×3 zero matrix is shown in Figure 1.3.

The *identity matrix* takes the place of the one in multiplication. Any matrix multiplied by the identity matrix will be exactly the same as the original matrix. The identity matrix is a square matrix that contains all zeros, with the exception of the diagonal. The diagonal elements starting at the top-left of the matrix and traveling to the bottom right contain ones instead of zeros. Why ones and zeros? The reason for this goes back to the definition of a matrix as a system of equations. The elements in a matrix represent the coefficients of that system. If you remember back to algebra again, when all of the coefficients in one of the equations is zero but one, it means you have solved for that variable. An identity matrix is just that. For each row or column there is a single "one," meaning the system of equations has been solved. Setting a matrix to the identity matrix essentially "resets" the matrix.

For example, if the matrix is being used to position geometry, such as the case with OpenGL's Modelview matrix, changing the matrix to the identity matrix (via glLoadIdentity() in OpenGL) will cause the next parts of the geometry received to be drawn relative to the origin again, rather than relative to the position specified by the previous matrix. Figure 1.3 shows the 3×3 identity matrix.

$$A = \begin{bmatrix} 0 & 0 & 0 \\ 0 & 0 & 0 \\ 0 & 0 & 0 \end{bmatrix} \quad I = \begin{bmatrix} 1 & 0 & 0 \\ 0 & 1 & 0 \\ 0 & 0 & 1 \end{bmatrix}$$

Figure 1.3   *The zero matrix and the identity matrices, both 3×3. They can be used as placeholders when you do not want to modify your original matrix. The identity matrix can also be used to reset transformations; anything transformed by the identity matrix will not be transformed at all.*

Matrix Operations

Now, on to the fun part, matrix math! As strange as matrices may seem, a majority of the mathematical operations that can be performed on them are relatively easy. Nearly everything that can be done with real numbers can be done with matrices as well.

Addition and Subtraction

Just like regular numbers, matrices can be added and subtracted. Matrix addition and subtraction are not used much in graphics programming, but that does not mean they cannot be used in other parts of your game. For instance, if you were building a strategy game, you could use a matrix to represent all of the remaining hitpoints of a group of units. You could add and subtract other matrices to or from this matrix to modify all of your unit's hitpoints at once, rather than messing with each unit individually. Given two matrixes, A and B, you simply take each element from A and add it to the corresponding element in B. The resulting value goes in the same element in the resultant matrix, called C. For instance, if A_{11} is 5 and B_{11} is 9, C_{11} would be 14. If we were subtracting A and B, then C_{11} would be negative 4.

Going back to the strategy game example, if A_{11} represented the hitpoints of "unit1" and B_{11} represented the number of hitpoints when the unit passed through a certain area on the screen, C_{11} would store the final number of hitpoints for "unit1". You could then run through the matrix and check for negative values, which would mean the unit is dead or disabled. Matrix addition is *associative*. This means, given three or more matrices, you can start by adding whichever two you like, without changing the final result. $(A + B) + C = A + (B + C)$. It is also *commutative*, meaning you can add and subtract matrices in any order without changing the result. $A + B = B + A$. An illustration of matrix addition is shown in Figure 1.4.

$$\begin{bmatrix} 3 & 5 & 0 \\ 4 & 4 & 8 \\ 9 & 6 & 1 \end{bmatrix} + \begin{bmatrix} 1 & 4 & 7 \\ 3 & 4 & 9 \\ 0 & 3 & 2 \end{bmatrix} = \begin{bmatrix} 3+1 & 5+4 & 0+7 \\ 4+3 & 4+4 & 8+9 \\ 9+0 & 6+3 & 1+2 \end{bmatrix} = \begin{bmatrix} 4 & 9 & 7 \\ 7 & 8 & 17 \\ 9 & 9 & 3 \end{bmatrix}$$

Figure 1.4 *An example of matrix addition using 3×3 matrices. Notice how each element of the first matrix is added to the corresponding element of the second matrix and the result is stored in the corresponding element of the final matrix.*

Scalar Multiplication

There are two types of matrix multiplication: matrix times matrix and matrix times scalar. Before you get into multiplying matrices by other matrices, you should perform scalar multiplication because it is much easier. A *scalar* is simply a number such as 10, 3, or 13,142. Multiplying or dividing a matrix by a scalar is quite easy. As always, you start with the matrix and a scalar value. All you need to do to multiply the whole matrix by your scalar is take each element, multiply it by the scalar, and place it in the resulting matrix. The same principle applies for scalar division. This operation is illustrated in Figure 1.5. A good use of this technique again goes back to the example used in the addition and subtraction section. Say your group of units takes a wrong turn and plows across a pit full of radioactive slime. This radioactive slime has the special property of removing half of the health from each unit in the group. Using scalar multiplication or division, you can perform this operation in one shot. Simply multiply the hitpoints matrix by 0.5 or divide it by 2.

$$4 \begin{bmatrix} 3 & 5 & 0 \\ 4 & 4 & 8 \\ 9 & 6 & 1 \end{bmatrix} \begin{bmatrix} 3 \times 4 & 5 \times 4 & 0 \times 4 \\ 4 \times 4 & 4 \times 4 & 8 \times 4 \\ 9 \times 4 & 6 \times 4 & 1 \times 4 \end{bmatrix} = \begin{bmatrix} 12 & 20 & 0 \\ 16 & 16 & 32 \\ 36 & 24 & 4 \end{bmatrix}$$

Figure 1.5   *Multiplying a matrix by a scalar (a constant number). Scalar multiplication will scale every element in the matrix by the same value.*

Matrix Multiplication

Okay, on to matrix multiplication! Lots of people get confused when it comes to multiplying matrices. In reality, however, it really isn't that hard. The first thing you need to do is determine whether the matrices are *conformable*. Lets say you have two matrices, A and B, that have the dimensions m×n and p×q. The matrices are conformable only if n=p. For instance, a 3×3 matrix and a 3×7 matrix can be multiplied together, but a 3×2 and a 4×5 matrix cannot. If your two matrices satisfy this requirement, you can move to the next step.

The resulting matrix will have the dimensions m×q. That means in the previous example, a 3×3 and a 3×7 matrix multiplied together would produce a 3×7 matrix. The nice thing about 3D graphics is that the matrices you use are usually square. When you multiply two square matrices together, you guessed it, you get a square matrix of the same size, so a 4×4 matrix multiplied by another 4×4 matrix will give you a final matrix with dimensions 4×4.

But just how do you multiply them together you ask? Well the idea is pretty simple. You take the first row of the first matrix and multiply it by the first column of the second matrix. This results in a single number that goes in the first row and first column of the result. The second element of the result is the first row of the first matrix times the second column of the second matrix, and so on. Sound confusing? Maybe you need to look at it a little differently.

Consider two 3×3 matrices, A and B, which are multiplied together to form C. You know that the first row of A contains the elements A_{11}, A_{12}, and A_{13}. The first column of B contains B_{11}, B_{21}, and B_{31}. In order to get C_{11}, you take $(A_{11} \times B_{11}) + (A_{12} \times B_{21}) + (A_{13} \times B_{31})$. You do that a total of nine times to get all the elements for the 3×3 result. Let's try multiplying one in Figure 1.6.

$$\begin{bmatrix} 3 & 5 & 0 \\ 4 & 4 & 8 \\ 9 & 6 & 1 \end{bmatrix} \begin{bmatrix} 2 & 5 & 2 \\ 7 & 3 & 1 \\ 4 & 5 & 9 \end{bmatrix} = \begin{bmatrix} 3\times2+5\times7+0\times4 & 3\times5+5\times3+0\times5 & 3\times2+5\times1+0\times9 \\ 4\times2+4\times7+8\times4 & 4\times5+4\times3+8\times5 & 4\times2+4\times1+8\times9 \\ 9\times2+6\times7+1\times4 & 9\times5+6\times3+1\times5 & 9\times2+6\times1+1\times9 \end{bmatrix} = \begin{bmatrix} 41 & 30 & 11 \\ 68 & 72 & 84 \\ 64 & 68 & 33 \end{bmatrix}$$

Figure 1.6   *Multiplying two matrices together. When multiplying matrices, you take the first row of A times the first row of B, the second row of A times the second column of B, and so on.*

CAUTION

Matrix multiplication is not *commutative*, meaning that unlike real numbers, the order in which you multiply two matrices *does* make a difference. If you have two matrices, A and B, multiplying A by B will not give you the same result as multiplying B by A (**AB ≠ BA**). Go ahead and try it with the matrices in Figure 1.6; the result is shown here:

$$\begin{bmatrix} 44 & 42 & 42 \\ 42 & 53 & 25 \\ 113 & 94 & 49 \end{bmatrix}$$

Determinants of Matrices

A *determinant* is a scalar value calculated from the elements of a matrix. Determinants of matrices are useful for many tasks, such as solving system's linear equations and calculating the area of a parallelogram or parallelepiped. You'll use determinants in game programming to calculate the inverse of a matrix. I will show you how to calculate the determinant, but I will not show you any of its applications, other than using it to find the inverse of a matrix.

The determinant of a 2×2 matrix is the easiest to calculate. All you need to do is multiply the top-left and bottom-right values together, and then subtract the product of the bottom-left and the top-right values as shown in Figure 1.7.

$$D = \begin{bmatrix} 1 & 5 \\ 7 & 3 \end{bmatrix} = 1 \times 3 - 5 \times 7 = -32$$

Figure 1.7   *Calculating the determinant of a 2×2 matrix. You need to know how to do this before you can calculate the determinates of matrices with dimensions greater than 2×2.*

Calculating the determinant of a 3×3 matrix is a bit harder. You first need to break the matrix into *minors*. To do this all you do is start at the first element in the first row. You eliminate the ith row and the jth column, and you are left with a 2×2 matrix. You multiply this matrix by the element that was used to calculate which row and column to delete. When you complete this process, you will be left with three 2×2 matrices. Next you need to calculate the determinant of each remaining matrix and add them together, as shown in Figure 1.8

$$D = \begin{bmatrix} 1 & 5 & 7 \\ 3 & 4 & 9 \\ 3 & 2 & 8 \end{bmatrix} = 1 \begin{bmatrix} 4 & 9 \\ 2 & 8 \end{bmatrix} - 5 \begin{bmatrix} 3 & 9 \\ 3 & 8 \end{bmatrix} + 7 \begin{bmatrix} 3 & 4 \\ 3 & 2 \end{bmatrix} =$$

$$1(4 \times 8 - 2 \times 9) - 5(3 \times 8 - 3 \times 9) + 7(3 \times 2 - 3 \times 4) =$$

$$14 - (-15) + (-42) = -13$$

Figure 1.8   *Calculating the determinant of a 3×3 matrix. You first break it into minors and use the definition of a 2×2 determinant to finish it off.*

The Inverse of a Matrix

Hey, what do you know, the last part of the matrix section is here already. That wasn't so bad was it? This section is on the inverse of a matrix. The inverse of a matrix satisfies the following equation: **M(M-1) = I.** M is the original matrix, M^{-1} is the inverse of M, and I is the identity matrix. In graphics programming, you could use the inverse of a transformation matrix to cancel out the effects of a previous transformation and return a previous transformation matrix. Not all matrices have an inverse. If a matrix is non-square or has a determinant of zero, it will not have an inverse. In programming it is important to make sure the matrix in question does have an inverse before performing this operation to prevent errors such as divide-by-zero. The inverse of a 3x3 matrix can be calculated as shown in Figure 1.9. In the figure M is the original matrix and the elements in the matrix shown are the cofactors of M, which I explain how to calculate here in a second.

$$\frac{1}{\det[M]} \begin{bmatrix} e_{11} & e_{12} & e_{13} \\ e_{21} & e_{22} & e_{23} \\ e_{31} & e_{32} & e_{33} \end{bmatrix}$$

Figure 1.9 *Calculating the inverse of a matrix. To calculate the inverse of a matrix, you first find its accompanying cofactor matrix, and then divide it by the determinant of the original matrix.*

In order to use that formula, you need to know how to calculate cofactors of the elements of the matrices. The principle is simple; you cross out the ith *column* and the jth *row*. Therefore, if the element is M_{11}, you would cross out the first row and the first column, leaving a 2×2 matrix . This is called the *minor* of the element. Now, you take the 2×2 matrix and calculate the determinant of it; the result of that determinant is called the *cofactor*. See Figure 1.10 for more details.

Now for the last step. Take your newly found cofactor matrix and multiply it by one over the determinant of the original matrix. The determinant in this case is –17, so you multiply the cofactor matrix by - 1/17. By doing this, you have the final inverted matrix, as shown in Figure 1.11.

$$M = \begin{bmatrix} 3 & 2 & 3 \\ 4 & 5 & 5 \\ 7 & 1 & 3 \end{bmatrix}$$

$$e_{11} = \begin{bmatrix} - & - & - \\ - & 5 & 5 \\ - & 1 & 3 \end{bmatrix} = \begin{bmatrix} 5 & 5 \\ 1 & 3 \end{bmatrix} = (5 \times 3 - 1 \times 5) = 10$$

$$e_{12} = \begin{bmatrix} - & 2 & 3 \\ - & - & - \\ - & 1 & 3 \end{bmatrix} = \begin{bmatrix} 3 & 2 \\ 3 & 1 \end{bmatrix} = (3 \times 1 - 3 \times 2) = -3$$

$$\begin{bmatrix} 10 & -3 & -5 \\ 23 & -12 & -3 \\ -31 & 11 & 7 \end{bmatrix}$$

Figure 1.10 *Calculating cofactors. Top: The original matrix.*
Middle: Calculating two of the cofactors. Bottom: The matrix with all its
cofactors calculated.

$$\frac{1}{-17} \begin{bmatrix} 10 & -3 & -5 \\ 23 & -12 & -3 \\ -31 & 11 & 7 \end{bmatrix} = \begin{bmatrix} -0.588 & 0.176 & 0.294 \\ -1.353 & 0.706 & 0.177 \\ 1.824 & -0.647 & -0.418 \end{bmatrix}$$

Figure 1.11 *Calculating the inverse of a matrix using the process*
described in the previous section—results are rounded to three decimal
places to save space.

Transposing Matrices

Transposing matrices is important in game programming because it is
a fast, easy way to calculate the inverse of orthogonal matrix. Now, let
your brain relax a bit; this operation is much easier. To transpose a

matrix all you have to do is take the columns of the matrix and make them the rows, and vice versa. The original matrix is *orthogonal* if when you multiply it by its transpose, you end with the identity matrix $(M(M^t) = I)$. As you know from the last function, a matrix multiplied by its inverse is also the identity matrix. It stands to reason that the transpose of the original matrix must also be its inverse. An example of an orthogonal matrix is the rotation matrix, which I will talk about later in the chapter. This is a piece of cake compared to matrix multiplication; just check out Figure 1.12.

$$A = \begin{bmatrix} 1 & 2 & 3 \\ 4 & 5 & 6 \\ 7 & 8 & 9 \end{bmatrix} \quad A^t = \begin{bmatrix} 1 & 4 & 7 \\ 2 & 5 & 8 \\ 3 & 6 & 9 \end{bmatrix}$$

Figure 1.12 *Left: The original matrix. Right: The matrix after it has been transposed. This is frequently done in game programming to find the inverse of rotation and other orthogonal matrices.*

Building Transformation Matrices

One of the most important uses for matrices in game programming is for transformations. Transformation matrices are used to position geometry and other objects onscreen. There are five main transformation matrices that you will use when working with 3D models. They are rotation around the X-axis, rotation around the Y-axis, rotation around the Z-axis, translation, and scaling. A rotation matrix, whether around the X, Y, or Z axes, will rotate all of the affected geometry around that specific axis. A translation matrix is used to move geometry from one place to another, and a scale matrix is used to change the size of the geometry.

The best thing about these matrices is the capability to multiply them together to perform several transformations with a single matrix. Keep in mind that the order of multiplication is important here; multiplying transformation matrices in one order will not necessarily give you the same result as multiplying the same matrices in a different order. Let's look at an example.

Say you have three rotation matrices. The first is a rotation of 90 degrees around the X-axis, the second -90 degrees around the X-axis, and the third a rotation of 90 degrees around the Y-axis. If you multiply them in the order of the first times the second, times the third, you will end with a rotation of 90 degrees around the Y-axis because the first two will cancel each other out. However, if you multiply in the order of the first times the third, times the second, your end result will be a positive 90 degree rotation around the Z-axis. Quite a difference.

So, how do you create these transformation matrices? Each rotation matrix will rotate a certain number of degrees around the X, Y, or Z axis. Figure 1.13 shows the X, Y, and Z rotation matrices.

$$
\begin{bmatrix}
1 & 0 & 0 & 0 \\
0 & \cos(\theta) & -\sin(\theta) & 0 \\
0 & \sin(\theta) & \cos(\theta) & 0 \\
0 & 0 & 0 & 1
\end{bmatrix}
\begin{bmatrix}
\cos(\theta) & 0 & -\sin(\theta) & 0 \\
0 & 1 & 0 & 0 \\
\sin(\theta) & 0 & \cos(\theta) & 0 \\
0 & 0 & 0 & 1
\end{bmatrix}
\begin{bmatrix}
\cos(\theta) & -\sin(\theta) & 0 & 0 \\
\sin(\theta) & \cos(\theta) & 0 & 0 \\
0 & 0 & 1 & 0 \\
0 & 0 & 0 & 1
\end{bmatrix}
$$

RotX   RotY   RotZ

Figure 1.13   The three rotation matrices. The left matrix is for rotation around the X axis, the center for rotation around the Y axis, the right for rotation around the Z axis. Each matrix will transform an object θ degrees around its respective axis. Note that they are placed in 4×4 matrices so they can be multiplied with the other transformation matrices, but they could be stored in a 3×3 matrix as well.

The translation matrix will move an object a set number of units in each direction. The distances in each direction are given by three values stored in the bottom row of the matrix. The scaling matrix is also very simple. Like the translation matrix, there are also three values, one for each axis. Instead of being in the bottom row of the matrix, they are located along the diagonal. The scaling matrix looks a lot like the identity matrix, only with values other than one in the diagonal. Figure 1.14 shows both the translation and the scaling matrices.

Using and Understanding Vectors

You know all about matrices now, so you can move on to the second concept, *vectors*. Vectors are one-dimensional arrays of numbers. In 3D graphics and games, most vectors have two, three, or even four components, one for each axis, but a vector can have as many components as needed. They can be used to represent locations, hold the direction and

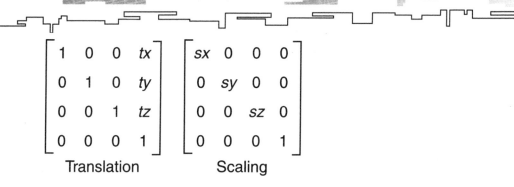

$$\begin{bmatrix} 1 & 0 & 0 & tx \\ 0 & 1 & 0 & ty \\ 0 & 0 & 1 & tz \\ 0 & 0 & 0 & 1 \end{bmatrix} \qquad \begin{bmatrix} sx & 0 & 0 & 0 \\ 0 & sy & 0 & 0 \\ 0 & 0 & sz & 0 \\ 0 & 0 & 0 & 1 \end{bmatrix}$$

Translation   Scaling

Figure 1.14 *The translation and scaling matrices. The translation matrix contains an ordered pair for movement along the X,Y, and Z axes; the scaling matrix contains an ordered pair for scaling along the X,Y, and Z axes.*

speed of movement of an object, and are used extensively when working with physics in 3D games.

A vector has both a magnitude and a direction. On paper, a vector can be drawn as an arrow. The length of the vector is its magnitude, and the arrowhead indicates the direction of the vector. In physics, you can represent the velocity of an object. The arrow points toward the direction the object was heading, and the length of the arrow indicates its speed. Figure 1.15 shows several examples of vectors.

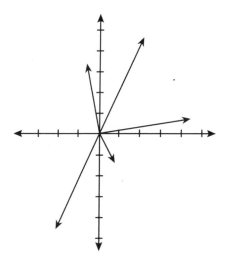

Figure 1.15 *A few vectors, each having its own magnitude and direction, on a two-dimensional graph. 2D, 3D, and 4D vectors are used extensively through game programming to represent character positions and movements, calculate how an object will react in an environment (physics), even store lighting information.*

Vector Notation

If you are going to understand how vectors work, you first must understand the notation that will be used whenever vectors are talked about. There are three ways of representing the vectors. The first is shown in the graphical method. The graphical method entails plotting the vectors on a set of axes. Although this works great if you need a visual representation of the vector, it is inconvenient to draw plot every time you want to talk about a vector. This method is often prone to error because it is hard to draw a vector the exact length and to the exact position. This error becomes worse when you try to draw three-dimensional vectors on a two-dimensional sheet of paper, and becomes impossible when you need to deal with vectors of four or more dimensions.

Fortunately, there are easier ways to represent vectors. The shortest and most common way uses the following notation:

⟨x,y,z⟩

where x, y, and z are the distances along the x, y, and z axes, respectively. When a vector is written using this notation it is called an *algebraic* vector. You will see much more of this notation later on in the chapter.

Magnitude and Unit Vectors

Vectors have a magnitude, usually depicted and thought about as length and written as ‖v‖, meaning the magnitude of the vector **v**, where **v** is any vector. As with a line segment, the length or magnitude of a vector can be found using the distance formula. The distance formula is shown in Figure 1.16. A unit vector is simply a vector with a magnitude of one. Any vector can be converted into a unit vector using the process of *normalization,* by dividing the vector by the vector's original magnitude. This is also shown in Figure 1.16.

Vector Arithmetic

You can perform all sorts of math with vectors. You can add them, subtract them, multiply them by *scalars* (constant numbers) to change their magnitude, and much more. This comes into play in

$$u = <3,4>$$

$$|u| = \sqrt{3^2 + 4^2} = 5$$

$$v = \frac{u}{|u|} = <0.6, 0.8>$$

$$|v| = \sqrt{0.6^2 + 0.8^2} = 1$$

Figure 1.16 *Finding the magnitude of a vector and using it to convert the original vector to a normal vector. Here, **v** is a vector that needs to be reduced down to a unit vector. As you can see, the current magnitude of **v** is 5. To calculate the unit vector **u** from **v** you divide each component of **v** by the magnitude of **v**, in this case 5. You can check it out at the end by calculating the magnitude of **u**; it should be 1.*

3D programming when you're moving players or other objects around onscreen. You use vectors to do this because vectors can store both the magnitude and direction, both of which are needed before you can calculate the new position of a player or object. This section covers vector arithmetic. You will learn how to work with vectors and how to do all of the basic vector operations needed for graphics programming.

Addition and Subtraction

As with real numbers and matrices you can add and subtract vectors. To add vectors together, you simply add the first component of the first vector to the first component of the second vector and so on. If you had a vector *<5,3>* and another vector *<1,2>* and you added them together, you would get a vector with the values *<6,5>*. This is illustrated in Figure 1.17.

Subtraction is accomplished the same way. Just take the values of the second vector and subtract them from the corresponding components in the first vector. So using the two vectors from the last section, *<5,3>* and *<1,2>*, you could subtract the second from the first and end up with the vector *<4,1>*. See Figure 1.18.

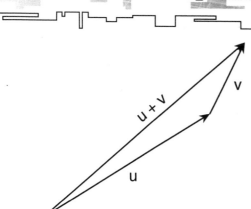

Figure 1.17 *Vectors can be added using the head to tail method. In this method, the first vector is drawn normally, but the second vector starts where the first ends. The vector that runs from the start of the first vector to the end of the second is called the resultant vector. Any number of vectors can be added this way, the resultant always being the vector between the start of the first vector and the end of the final one.*

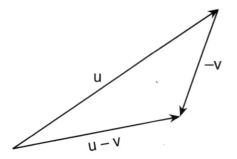

Figure 1.18 *Vector subtraction can be performed the same way as vector addition with one minor change. When you draw the vectors, the vector you are subtracting should go the opposite way as it normally would.*

Scalar Multiplication and Division

Just like matrices, you can multiply and divide vectors by scalar values. This is useful when you want to scale the speed of a vehicle up or down, or enlarge a picture. For instance, if you had an object moving at a certain speed in a certain direction and you wanted to make it go twice as fast in the same direction, you would multiply its movement vector by a scalar. The principle you use is much the same as the one you used for matrices. All you need to do is multiply each component of the vector by the scalar. Check out Figure 1.19 for a visual representation.

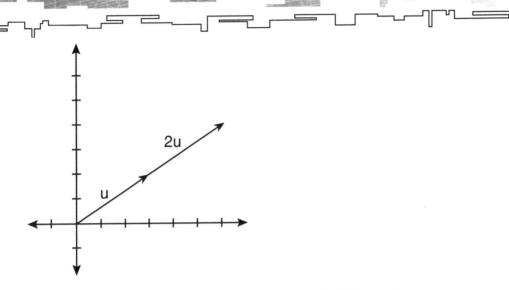

Figure 1.19 *Scalar multiplication of vectors. A vector multiplied by a scalar will have the same direction as the original, but a different magnitude (length).*

Vector Products

Vectors cannot be multiplied together in the traditional sense. Instead of standard multiplication, there are two operations that take its place—the *dot product* (also known as the scalar product) and the *cross product* (also known as the vector product).

The Dot (or Scalar) Product

The dot product can be used to find the angle between two vectors and is a quick test to determine whether two vectors are orthogonal (at right angles to each other). This can be useful in 3D programming if you need to find the final direction and speed of an object that has wind, gravity, or other forces acting upon it. You would only need to know the direction and magnitude of the forces, and the direction the object would move without the extra force acting on it.

Two vectors are orthogonal to each other if their dot product is zero. The dot product is defined in two ways. The first is **u•v = ||u||*||v||*cosθ**. The second way is **u•v = i1i2 + j1j2 ... n1n2**. All this means is that you multiply each of the vector components in the first vector by the corresponding component in the second vector, and then add all the results. The first equation (**u•v = ||u||*||v||*cosθ**) is used when you only know the magnitudes and angle between the two vectors, but may not know the actual values of each component. The second equation (**u•v** = i1i2 + j1j2 ... n1n2) is used when you do not know the angle between your two vectors, only the vector's components. So now how do you use those definitions to find the angle between your two vectors? Simple, you just call up your algebra and trig skills and solve the first equation for *theta*, which stands for the angle between the vectors. This is done for you in Figure 1.20. As always an example is shown as well.

$$u \bullet v = |u||v|\cos\theta$$

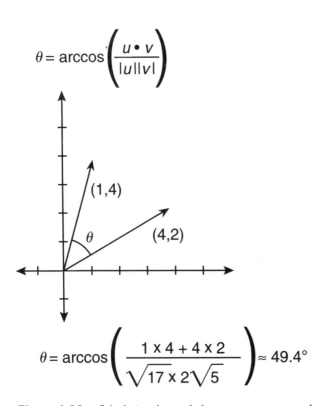

$$\theta = \arccos\left(\frac{u \bullet v}{|u||v|}\right)$$

$$\theta = \arccos\left(\frac{1 \times 4 + 4 \times 2}{\sqrt{17} \times 2\sqrt{5}}\right) \approx 49.4°$$

Figure 1.20 *Calculating the angle between two vectors, don't forget to use the second definition for the dot product. The first part shows the equation for the dot product solved for theta (the angle between the two vectors). Don't forget that ||v|| means the magnitude of **v**. The second part shows the calculations involved in calculating the angle between two vectors using the vectors <1,4> and <4,2>.*

The Cross (or Vector) Product

The *cross product* can also be useful. Calculating the cross product of two vectors yields a vector that is perpendicular to both of them. This can be used to find vectors that are normal, or perpendicular, to a surface. This is done often in 3D programming to calculate the lighting normals. The normals used for lighting purposes are unit vectors that must be perpendicular to the surface that is being lit. The cross product comes in handy when trying to find these values.

The cross product equation expands to the following: **u×v = (y1z2-z1y2)i-(x1z2-z1x2)j+(x1y2-y1x2)k** where *i*, *j*, and *k* are the vector components for the *x*, *y*, and *z* axes, respectively. As you noticed, it will not work on two-dimensional vectors, so three-dimensional vectors are used instead.

Check out Figure 1.21 for an example.

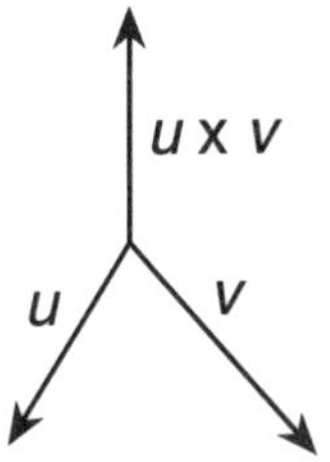

$$\langle 1,5,2 \rangle \times \langle 2,1,3 \rangle$$

$$(5 \times 3 - 2 \times 1)i - (1 \times 3 - 2 \times 2)j + (1 \times 1 - 5 \times 2)k =$$

$$\langle 13,1,-9 \rangle$$

Figure 1.21   *Calculating the cross product. The resultant vector will be orthogonal (perpendicular) to both of the vectors used in its calculation. You can verify this by taking the dot product of each of the vectors by the result. You will find you get a value of 0, meaning the vectors are orthogonal, both times.*

Transforming a Vector by a Matrix

Often in computer graphics and game programming, you will need to use matrices to move vectors and points around onscreen, such as to move a point or piece of geometry to a new position. This process is called *transformation*. Matrices are used here for two reasons. First, they are excellent ways to store transformations as you saw previously, and second, they can easily be used to transform vectors and points by multiplication.

In order to transform a vector, you simply use the vector as a 3×1 or 4×1 matrix, depending on which type of matrix you are using to transform. This is important because if you try to multiply a 3×1 matrix with a 4×4 matrix, it will not work. The same goes for a 4×1 matrix being multiplies with a 3×3. Do not worry if your vector does not fill the whole matrix, for instance a 3D vector being transformed by a 4×4 matrix. All you need to do is set the last element in the 4×1 matrix to 1. Then, after transformation, the last value can be discarded and you will once again have a vector with the same number of dimensions that you started with. Multiply your matrices together, and you will get a new, transformed, vector. This operation is shown in Figure 1.22.

$$\begin{bmatrix} 1 & 2 & 3 \\ 4 & 5 & 6 \\ 7 & 8 & 9 \end{bmatrix} \begin{bmatrix} 3 \\ 1 \\ 4 \end{bmatrix} = \begin{bmatrix} 1 \times 3 + 2 \times 1 + 3 \times 4 \\ 4 \times 3 + 5 \times 1 + 6 \times 4 \\ 7 \times 3 + 8 \times 1 + 9 \times 4 \end{bmatrix} = \begin{bmatrix} 17 \\ 41 \\ 65 \end{bmatrix}$$

Figure 1.22   *Transforming a vector by a matrix. Multiplying a vector by a matrix will yield a new vector with a new, transformed position. The operation is just regular matrix multiplication as defined earlier in the chapter, only this time it isn't using two square matrices.*

The CD's Code

Take a look at the following directory on the CD: /Code/Chapter1/ or /Code/Math. Here, you will find C++ classes to store and manipulate matrices and vectors. There are separate classes for 3×3 and 4×4 matrices, both defined and implemented in the files matrix.cpp and matrix.inl. The same goes for vectors. There are classes for both 2D and 3D vectors, defined and implemented in vector.h and vector.inl. All of the classes contain a variety of functions to perform the operations covered here, as well as overloaded operators that can be used to do the basic mathematical operations such as addition and subtraction. There are even operators to compare two matrices or vectors and tell you if they are equal. All these operators allow you to use matrices and vectors as if you were just using real numbers. Syntax such as vector1 = vector2 + vector3 and if(matrix1 == matrix2) are both valid thanks to the wonderful features of C++ that allow programmers to override the default definition of the mathematical operators.

In both directories you will notice a few extra files, as follows:

- math.h is the main header file that basically includes all of the other files, ensuring that you get all of the functionality available, without needing to remember to include a bunch of files.

- The other two files, quaternion.h and quaternion.inl, are the definitions and implementation of a class that is used to store and manipulate *quaternions*, which you will be learning about in the next chapter. There are a few functions in the matrix and vector classes that use quaternions, generally signified by taking either a reference to a CQuaternion class as a parameter, or returning a CQuaternion class. Don't panic if you don't know what these functions are for; you will learn about them in the next chapter.

Conclusion

That concludes the brief review of matrix and vector math. If you need or want to learn more about either, I suggest that you visit a local college library or bookstore and pick yourself up a book on linear algebra. The books I used as a reference for most of this were *Matrices*, written by Frank Ayres Jr. and *Linear Algebra*, by the same author. Both are part of a series of math references known as Schaum's Outlines Series of Mathematics. If you cannot afford a book, or simply want a different solution, I once again suggest Eric Weisstein's *World of Mathematics*, available at http://mathworld.wolfram.com. Eric Weisstein's *World of Mathematics* has examples and explanations for many mathematical problems, including matrices and vectors.

The next chapter introduces you to *quaternions*. Quaternions are used by graphics programmers to represent rotations, much like a 3×3 rotation matrix. However, quaternions hold several advantages over traditional matrices, such as the capability to avoid *gimbal lock*, and the capability to create easy, smooth interpolation between orientations. To top it all off, they take up less space than matrices. Check it out!

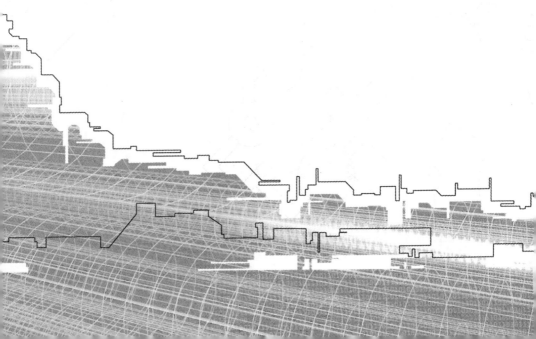

CHAPTER 2

Introduction to Quaternions

A s you explore the wide world of three-dimensional graphics, you will journey past vectors and matrices into the land of the quaternion. You may have heard this word thrown around before, but you may not know what it means. That is what this chapter is for. By the time you finish this chapter, you should have a decent understanding of what a quaternion is, how they work, what they are good for, and why you should use them.

What Is a Quaternion and Why Are They Used?

Quaternions comprise a set of four numbers that are used to represent rotations. Consider three-dimensional rotation, rotation in three-dimensional space, discussed in Chapter 1, add one more dimension, and you end up with a four-dimensional rotation. There are two components in each quaternion, a vector component which consists of x, y, and z values, and a scalar value which is usually denoted as w. The scalar value represents the angle of rotation in the form cos(angle / 2).

Quaternions can also be written as a scalar value such as n followed by a bold letter representing a vector. For example, =q = [n**v**].

I can already see that you are thinking, "why the heck would I need something like that?" To understand why you might need

> **NOTE**
>
> Euler angles are probably the most familiar, and in most cases, the most practical way to represent the orientation of an object. A set of three Euler angles specifies the rotation around each axis, **X**, **Y**, and **Z**. For example, you might use Euler angles to represent the orientation of an airplane in your flight simulator. Rotations around each axis are called roll, pitch, and yaw; the axis each is associated with varies depending on the coordinate system and the applications.

quaternions, you first must learn a bit about another important part of 3D graphics, Euler angles, which are discussed in more detail later in this chapter.

There are several reasons you should use quaternions to rotate your objects and characters in your games. The first, and most important, advantage is the fact that quaternions are not susceptible to gimbal lock, a phenomenon in which an object loses the ability to rotate on one of its three axes. Gimbal lock shows its face when two axes point in the same direction. This causes all sorts of problems. See Figure 2.1 for a picture of gimbal lock.

Another advantage to quaternions is the ability to have smooth, interpolated rotations. It is much easier to interpolate rotations using quaternions rather than matrices, resulting in smoother animations. The last main advantage of using quaternions is they take less room than a rotation matrix (four elements versus nine), and some operations are cheaper to perform on quaternions in terms of processor cycles.

Even though quaternions have many advantages over matrices, keep in mind that most graphics APIs will not accept quaternions directly. They must first be converted into matrices, a process that takes a fair amount of CPU cycles. Keep this in mind when deciding whether you are going to use quaternions in your game engine.

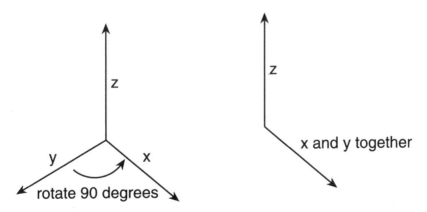

Figure 2.1 *When two axes point in the same direction, you get gimbal lock. When you use quaternions for rotations, you avoid any possibility of gimbal lock occurring.*

W.R Hamilton

W.R Hamilton created quaternions in 1843, in Dublin, England. Originally used as a four-dimensional extension for complex numbers, it was proven that quaternions could be used to represent rotations in three-dimensional space as well.

Quaternion Operations

Quaternions can be treated simply as four-dimensional vectors for the purposes of addition, subtraction, and scalar multiplication. Quaternion addition is exactly the same as vector addition, meaning you simply add the components of the first quaternion to the corresponding components of the second one. The same is true for subtraction, although of course you subtract the components instead of add them.

Scalar multiplication of quaternions also follows the same path as vectors. Each of the four components in the quaternion is multiplied by the scalar. Figure 2.2 shows an example of both addition and scalar multiplication.

$$q = [1 \ 2 \ 3 \ 4] \quad p = [5 \ 6 \ 7 \ 8]$$
$$q + p = [6 \ 8 \ 10 \ 12]$$
$$2p = [2 \ 4 \ 6 \ 8]$$

Figure 2.2 *An example of quaternion addition and scalar multiplication. Although not used directly in 3D programming, both of these operations are needed later, when you interpolate between two quaternions.*

Two other important qualities quaternions share with vectors is the way their magnitude is calculated, and the way a unit quaternion is calculated. As with vectors, to calculate the magnitude of a quaternion, you square each component of the quaternion, add them all together, and take the square root of the result.

A quaternion does not become a "rotation quaternion" (a quaternion representing a rotation) unless it is a unit quaternion. A unit quaternion is the same as a unit vector. A unit quaternion has a magnitude of exactly one, no more, no less. You can convert any quaternion to a unit quaternion by dividing each of the components by the total magnitude.

Unless your quaternion has a magnitude of one, it does not represent a rotation. If you find yourself with a quaternion without a magnitude of one, other than in the middle of an interpolation, you have probably done something wrong.

Multiplying Quaternions

As you read in the first part of this chapter, some operations that are normally performed on matrices can be done much cheaper with quaternions. One of these is multiplication. Multiplying two quaternions together has the same effect as multiplying their corresponding rotation matrices, but at a lower computational cost. Multiplying two rotation quaternions will cause the rotations to become *concatenated*, or strung together in a series. For example, if one rotation represents a rotation around the X axis and another rotation matrix represents a rotation around the Y axis, multiplying them together will create a matrix that represents a rotation around the X and Y axes. The formula for quaternion multiplication is shown in Figure 2.3.

$$p = [m,u] \quad q = [n,v]$$

$$qp = [mn - v \bullet u, nu + mv + (v \times u)]$$

Figure 2.3 *In the quaternion multiplication formula,* n *and* m *are the scalar components of the quaternion, and* u *and* v *are the vector components. Note:* • *refers to the dot product of the two vectors, whereas* × *refers to the cross product of two vectors.*

Calculating the Conjugate of a Quaternion

The *conjugate* of a quaternion is used for operations such as rotation of a quaternion by another or rotation of a vector by a quaternion. This is especially useful when you are transforming lighting normals or other operations whereby translation is not needed.

The conjugate is very easy to calculate, requiring only that you negate the vector component of the quaternion. Therefore, if you have the quaternion q = [n,v], where *n* is a scalar and *v* is a vector, the conjugate of *q* (denoted by the symbol ~) would be ~q = [n, -v]. You will learn how to use the conjugate of a quaternion to rotate other quaternions and vectors in the next section.

Rotating a Quaternion

You can use quaternions to rotate vectors or other quaternions. The same formula is used to rotate quaternions by other quaternions as to rotate vectors by other quaternions. The only difference is that the vector becomes a quaternion with a scalar component of zero, yet the scalar of the resulting product is ignored. The formula for rotating vectors and quaternions is shown in Figure 2.4.

$$p' = q(p)(\sim q)$$

p can be a quarternion or a vector

Figure 2.4 *Using a quaternion to rotate vectors and other quaternions. Remember, when rotating a vector, you use a quaternion with a scalar value of zero and ignore the resulting scalar in the result.*

Quaternion Conversions

Because of the complicated nature of quaternions, it is not always feasible to specify a quaternion rotation directly. Instead, you might want to specify a set of three Euler angles, or perhaps a rotation around an arbitrary axis, particularly if you need to retrieve input from a user. An average human being would have a hard time trying to enter a rotation quaternion and would much rather enter a set of Euler angles. For purposes of transforming vertices or other game components, you may require a rotation matrix instead of a quaternion. This is no problem; you can convert between all of these elements with very little effort. The next section begins with quaternion to matrix conversion.

Converting Between Matrices and Quaternions

One of the most important aspects of quaternions is their ability to be converted into rotation matrices. This is useful because graphics APIs such as OpenGL and Direct3D cannot accept quaternions directly rather, they rely on matrices to perform transformations. Because of this, without being able to convert between quaternions, your graphics would become useless because you would not be able to use the information they contain along with OpenGL or other graphics APIs. For example, if you have two sets of rotations for an object, the first set is the starting rotation and the second is the ending rotation. Without being able to convert these matrices to quaternions, it would be impossible to take advantage of the ease of interpolation between quaternions. Keep in mind that all matrices will be referenced in the manner mij where i is the row and j is the column.

This section first investigates how to convert a quaternion to a matrix. Because there is much more to cover in the later chapters of the book, there is not room to go through the "whys" of the conversion. Instead, this section looks at the formula for the conversion. Figure 2.5 shows how to generate a 3×3 rotation matrix from a quaternion. Keep in mind that when writing code to do the conversion, it is helpful to calculate some of the multiplication ahead of time to avoid unnecessary overhead.

$$\begin{bmatrix} w^2 + x^2 - y^2 - z^2 & 2xy - 2wz & 2xz + 2yn \\ 2xy + 2wz & w^2 - x^2 + y^2 - z^2 & 2yz - 2wx \\ 2xz - 2wy & 2yz - 2wx & w^2 - x^2 - y^2 + z^2 \end{bmatrix}$$

Figure 2.5 *Converting a quaternion to a rotation matrix. W represents the scalar value and X, Y, and Z represent the three parts of the vector component.*

Converting back to a quaternion is a little bit harder, but not much. The first thing you do is calculate the trace of the matrix using the formula (tr = m11+m22+m33). If that value comes out to be greater than zero, you can perform an "instant calculation" using the following formula:

$$temp = \frac{1}{2\sqrt{tr + 1}}$$

$$q_w = \frac{0.25}{temp}$$

$$q_x = (m_{23} - m_{32}) \times temp$$

$$q_y = (m_{31} - m_{13}) \times temp$$

$$q_z = (m_{12} - m_{21}) \times temp$$

If it is less than or equal to zero, you have to take a different approach that depends on which element of the major diagonal is the largest. If the upper-left corner is the largest, you use this formula:

$$temp = \frac{1}{2\sqrt{1 + m_{11} - m_{22} + m_{33}}}$$

$$q_w = \frac{0.25}{temp}$$

$$q_x = (m_{21} + m_{12}) \times temp$$

$$q_y = (m_{13} + m_{31}) \times temp$$

$$q_z = (m_{32} - m_{23}) \times temp$$

If the middle element outshines the others, use this formula:

$$temp = \frac{1}{\sqrt{1 + m_{22} - m_{11} - m_{33}}}$$

$$q_w = (m_{21} + m_{12}) \times temp$$

$$q_x = \frac{0.25}{temp}$$

$$q_y = (m_{32} + m_{23}) \times temp$$

$$q_z = (m_{13} - m_{31}) \times temp$$

And finally, if the lower-right corner takes the cake, use this one:

$$temp = \frac{1}{\sqrt{1 + m_{33} - m_{11} - m_{22}}}$$

$$q_w = (m_{13} + m_{31}) \times temp$$

$$q_x = (m_{32} + m_{23}) \times temp$$

$$q_y = \frac{0.25}{temp}$$

$$q_z = (m_{21} - m_{12}) \times temp$$

These formulas convert your rotation matrix into a quaternion so you can take advantage of the many advantages they have, such as easy interpolation, cheaper multiplication, and less storage space.

Converting Between Euler Angles and Quaternions

There is one huge reason that conversion between Euler angles and quaternions is necessary—ease of use. Because it is impossible to visualize a quaternion, it is very hard to enter one into a program. If a modeling program wants you to input a rotation value for an object, it would be considerably easier to enter three Euler angles rather than to enter a quaternion.

To convert a set of Euler angles to a quaternion, you first must convert each angle to its own quaternion. This is done using one of three formulas, depending on which axis your rotation is around. All three formulas are shown in the second part of Figure 2.6. To create a final quaternion, all you have to do is multiply the three previous quaternions.

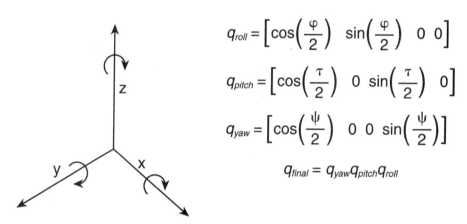

$$q_{roll} = \left[\cos\left(\frac{\varphi}{2}\right) \quad \sin\left(\frac{\varphi}{2}\right) \quad 0 \quad 0 \right]$$

$$q_{pitch} = \left[\cos\left(\frac{\tau}{2}\right) \quad 0 \quad \sin\left(\frac{\tau}{2}\right) \quad 0 \right]$$

$$q_{yaw} = \left[\cos\left(\frac{\psi}{2}\right) \quad 0 \quad 0 \quad \sin\left(\frac{\psi}{2}\right) \right]$$

$$q_{final} = q_{yaw}q_{pitch}q_{roll}$$

Figure 2.6 *Left: A representation of Euler angles. Right: Converting the three Euler angles into quaternions.*

When you are ready to convert a quaternion, you must call on the miracle of quaternion to matrix conversion. Before you can do anything else, you must calculate certain elements of the rotation matrix, which will later be used to extract the angles.

The elements you need to calculate are m11, m21, m31, m32, and m33. Let's review how to acquire those five elements from a quaternion.

$$m_{11} = w^2 + x^2 - y^2 - z^2$$
$$m_{21} = 2xy + 2wz$$
$$m_{31} = 2xz - 2wy$$
$$m_{32} = 2yx + 2wx$$
$$m_{33} = w^2 - x^2 - y^2 + z^2$$

Now all that is left is to extract the angles. Once those figures are calculated, you can extract the Euler angles using the following formulas:

$$roll = \arctan\left(\frac{m_{32}}{m_{33}}\right)$$

$$pitch = \arcsin(-m_{31})$$

$$yaw = \arctan\left(\frac{m_{21}}{m_{11}}\right)$$

These formulas are very useful. Most people would balk if a program displayed quaternions instead of Euler angles to represent a rotation. They would be much happier to simply see the three direction angles instead because they can visualize the rotation much easier. With these equations you can still appreciate all the advantages of quaternions without driving away the people using your program.

Axis-Angle Conversions

The last kind of conversion you will learn about in this chapter converts a rotation angle and axis to a quaternion. You'll need to do this because most graphics APIs cannot use a quaternion to directly represent a rotation, so when the time comes to apply the rotation, the quaternion must be converted to another form. It might be possible to simply rotate around an axis using a function such as glRotate, rather than build a complete rotation matrix. Because there are fewer operations involved in converting from a quaternion to an axis angle than converting from a quaternion to a rotation matrix, the axis-angle approach may be a better choice when available.

This is by far the easiest conversion of the three. The left side of Figure 2.7 shows how axis-angle rotation can be represented in three dimensions. The angle is a rotation around an arbitrary axis, generally represented by a unit vector. To convert your axis/angle pair to a quaternion, you first must make sure that your axis is a unit vector. If it is, you calculate `sin(angle / 2)` and divide all the components of the axis by it before storing them in the vector component of the destination quaternion. The scalar part of the quaternion is calculated using the formula `cos(angle / 2)`. Simple enough? Check out the right side of Figure 2.7 if you are still a little bit confused.

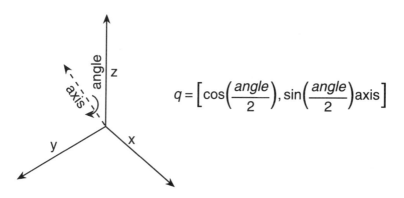

$$q = \left[\cos\left(\frac{angle}{2}\right), \sin\left(\frac{angle}{2}\right) axis \right]$$

Figure 2.7 *Left: A picture axis-angle rotation. Right: Converting the axis and angle to a quaternion.*

Converting back is not hard at all. Using the inverse trig functions to reverse the earlier operations and one of the most basic trig identities, you can easily extract the rotation angle and axis. Step right over to Figure 2.8 to see how to do it.

$$sa = \sqrt{1 - q_w^2}$$

$$angle = 2\arccos(q_w)$$

$$axis_x = \frac{q_x}{sa}$$

$$axis_y = \frac{q_y}{sa}$$

$$axis_z = \frac{q_z}{sa}$$

Figure 2.8 *Converting a quaternion to a rotation axis and angle. This conversion is cheaper in terms of processing power than a quaternion-to-matrix conversion, making it ideal for use when a rotation matrix is not necessary and when the graphics API can accept a rotation in the axis-angle format.*

Interpolation with Quaternions

Now, after all that, you get to learn about the coolest thing in quaternions: interpolation. Interpolation is very important when working with 3D models. Imagine that you are working on a game that includes enemies who patrol an area, back and forth. All you have to work with are the endpoints of the patrol path and the time it should take for the enemy to get from one to the other. This poses a problem because you don't actually know the points where the enemy would be at any given time. Using interpolation, you can calculate where the enemies should be, no matter how much time has elapsed since they started patrolling.

Interpolation is the act of producing the points in between two end points. This can help produce smooth animation because you can generate an unlimited number of midpoints, allowing the jumps between points to be very small and—hopefully—imperceptible to your game players. Interpolation is the real reason you should be using quaternions. It is pretty easy to use and it results in super-smooth animation. In this section, you will learn about the two main types of quaternion interpolation: LERP and SLERP. Linear interpolation (LERP) interpolates in a straight line. Spherical linear interpolation (SLERP), on the other hand, interpolates in an arc. SLERP generally produces a smoother animation, and will always stay at a constant speed, whereas a LERPed animation will tend to speed up in the middle and slow down at the ends. Figure 2.9 shows a two-dimensional sketch of SLERP and LERP.

In general, you want to use SLERP to interpolate between two sets of rotations. This allows the path to actually rotate, rather than simply be connected by a straight line. Unfortunately, SLERP becomes unreliable as the distance between the rotations becomes smaller. When this is the case, you must fall back to LERP (see Figure 2.9).

Notice in the figure that the intervals are all the same size on the SLERP path, but are close together toward the middle of the LERP path. This is why SLERP is used for rotation interpolation in most places; it simply looks better. Now, you'll learn how to actually perform these operations on quaternions in the next sections.

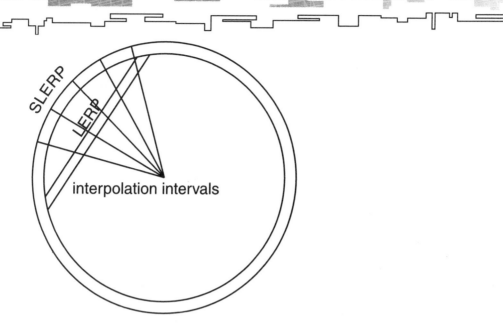

Figure 2.9 *A 2D representation of what SLERP and LERP do. SLERP interpolates along the arc of the circle, whereas LERP interpolates along a straight line from start to finish.*

LERP (Linear Interpolation of Quaternions)

Linear interpolation is by far the easier of the two methods. Figure 2.10 shows the formula to linearly interpolate two quaternions, called q and p, using an interpolation value of t, which is between zero and one. After performing the operations, you must be sure to convert the resulting quaternion back to a unit quaternion, or the end result will not be what you expect.

$$LERP(q,p,t) = t(p - q) + q$$

Figure 2.10 *The equation to linearly interpolate (LERP) between two quaternions. The path between the two quaternions will be a straight line.*

SLERP (Spherical Linear Interpolation)

Spherical linear interpolation is not all that hard either. The only thing you have to watch out for is making sure you take the shortest route. If you look at Figure 2.9 again, you will see that you could go the short way, as the figure shows, or you could go back around the long way. Most things would look pretty funny if you chose to interpolate the long way. Taking the long route would be like turning right at an intersection by turning left for three quarters of a turn and then turning right. Imagine how strange that would look to a bystander. You can make sure it always takes the shortest arc by checking the dot product of the two quaternions, and negating one if necessary. See the code on the included CD for details; you will find it in the /Code/Math and Code/Chapter2 directories in the files quaternion.h and quaternion.inl. On to the SLERP formula! Figure 2.11 shows you how to SLERP between two quaternions. Again, *t* is a value between zero and one.

$$SLERP(q,p,t) = \frac{q\sin(\theta(1-t)) + p\sin(\theta t)}{\sin(\theta)}$$

Figure 2.11 *The formula for using interpolating between two quaternions using the SLERP method. Unlike LERP, where the resulting path will be a line, the resulting path of SLERP is an arc.*

Conclusion

There you have it, the basic operations of quaternions. Hopefully you now have enough information to get some use out of them. Throughout the next few chapters, you will use them to provide smooth animation for your 3D models. If you desire to learn more about the background and the math behind quaternions, I would suggest picking up book devoted solely to them. W.R. Hamilton published several on his discovery, and many people have devoted manuscripts to quaternions as well. Just search your favorite online bookstore (most "physical" bookstores do not carry books such as these) and see what you find. There are also many online resources and sites that cover the ins and outs of quaternions. Load up your favorite Internet search engine and search away.

That concludes the math section. Next up, you will begin to learn about 3D model formats. The book starts with simple formats such as Alias|Wavefront's Object format (OBJ) and id Software's MD2 format, originally created for *Quake II*. The book then moves on to more complicated formats, such as MilkShape 3D's MS3D and id Software's MD3 format.

CHAPTER 3

Quake II's MD2 Models

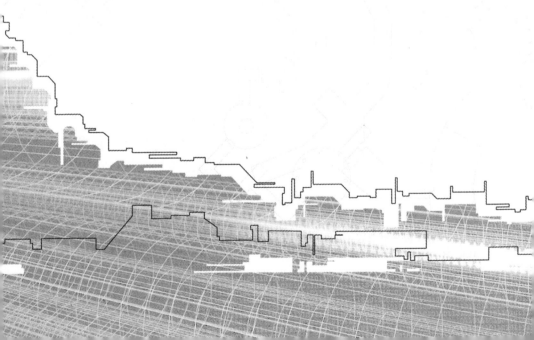

F inally, you are through all that math and introductory stuff. Now, on to the first chapter that really deals with 3D models!

First up, the MD2 format. The MD2 format was created by the folks at id Software for the hit game, *Quake II* (see Figure 3.1). Since then, the MD2 format has become a popular format for aspiring game developers due to its simple, easy-to-use format, the availability of quality tools with which to create models, and the large collection of fan-built models available at sites such as http://www.polycount.com. MD2 models can be used in your game for just about anything. Enemies, weapons, pickups, even pieces of the world geometry such as crates and light fixtures can be stored using this format.

Figure 3.1 *id Software's Quake II introduced the MD2 format. Throughout the game all the enemies, pickups, and weapons were stored in this format. Here, one of the monsters (stored in the MD2 format of course) from the game harasses the player.*

From here on, I am assuming that you are familiar with basic file I/O routines, specifically the ones in the standard C library (FILE *, fread, fwrite, and so on). If you're not, you definitely want to brush up on them before you continue. A large part of loading 3D models is getting them loaded into memory correctly. Any good C book should have a detailed section on these functions, but you get an introduction right here in this chapter!

Understanding the FILE * Functions

One of the most important parts of model loading is just getting the file into memory. One of the ways to do this is to use a set of functions from the standard C library, collectively known as the FILE * functions. You have probably heard of them, perhaps even used them before. This section is intended to give you a basic overview of the most important functions and datatypes used for I/O. The first thing you need to do before you can use FILE * I/O is include the appropriate header. You will need <stdio.h> for C programming or <cstdio> for C++.

The first and most important part of the FILE* I/O is not a function at all. Rather, it is a datatype called FILE. FILE is always used as a pointer (FILE *) and holds exactly what it sounds like, a pointer to the file called a *file pointer*. You need a separate file pointer for each file you want to have open; each file pointer can only point to a single file at a time.

So now you have a datatype that points to the file, but how do you use it? The first thing you need to do is open a file. The function you want here is fopen(). fopen takes just two parameters. The first is a constant string (const char *) that contains the file name of the file you desire to open, the second, also a constant string (const char *), is the mode you want to open the file in. The mode parameter can take many forms, depending on what you want to do with the file. There are modes for reading, and writing, and binary and text files.

How do you determine which mode to use? Simple, just check Tables 3.1 and 3.2 for a list of all the mode strings that can be used with fopen. The mode string will consist of one part from Table 3.1, which tells fopen which type of access you want, whether it be reading, writing, appending, or a combination. The second part of the mode string comes from Table 3.2. The second part, also known as the *translation mode,* tells fopen whether to look at it as a binary or text file.

The fopen function will return the file pointer (FILE *) for your file. This file pointer will be used whenever you work with the file, whether it is to read data from it or write new data back. Here are a few examples of opening a file in different modes:

```
FILE * f = fopen("file.txt", "w+t");
```

This will create and open the file called file.txt for reading and writing in text mode. Anything currently contained within file.txt will be destroyed.

```
FILE * f = fopen("file.bin", "rb");
```

Table 3.1 Access Modes for fopen()

Mode String	Use
"r"	Opens the file for reading only. If the file does not exist, a new one will not be created and the call to fopen will fail.
"w"	Opens a blank file for writing. If the target file contains information, it is wiped out. Be careful when using this mode; you could wipe out a file.
"a"	Opens a file for writing, much the same as the "w" mode. However, "a" will not destroy the data in the file. Any new data will be added to the end of the file, also known as *appending* the data.
"r+"	Opens an existing file for reading and writing. As with "r", the file must exist or fopen will fail.
"w+"	Works the same as "r+" with two major differences. If the file does not exist, fopen will create a blank one. If the file does exist, all data will be erased. Another function to be careful with.
"a+"	Opens the file for both reading and appending, or writing to the end of the file.

Table 3.2 Translation Modes for fopen()

Mode String	Use
"t"	"t" stands for text mode. In text mode, each byte of the file will be treated as its own character. You will generally use this format if the file was or needs to be human-readable.
"b"	"b" is for binary. A file opened in binary mode will be treated as raw data and is generally not human-readable.

This will open the file file.bin for reading only, in binary mode. This is the most common mode used when loading and using 3D models within your games for several reasons. First, most model files are in binary form (but not all of them; the next chapter contains a file format that is text-based). Second, you rarely need to write to a model file when working with it in your game. Generally, you only need to load and use, rather than modify, the data it contains. Don't forget to determine whether your file pointer is valid (not zero) before you try to use it.

Now that you have an open file, you need to be able to retrieve data from it. When working with model files, I like to read in the whole file as a chunk of unformatted data, and then sort it out later. To do this you use fread().

fread is used for just what it sounds like: *file reading*. This function reads raw, unformatted data into an array. This is a quick and easy way to get data from the file into memory. The fopen function takes four parameters, as follows:

- The first parameter is a pointer to a buffer in which to store the new data.

- The second and third parameters will tell fread how much data you want. These parameters contain the number of bytes in a single "item," or chunk, of data, and the number of items you would like to read, respectively. Be sure your buffer is large enough to hold all of your data; nothing is worse than overwriting an array and losing data.

- The fourth and final parameter is a file pointer. The parameter should contain the file pointer that you created when you opened the file using fopen. You can check fread to make sure it read everything. The fread function returns the number of items actually read. If this return value and the third parameter of fread are equal, all the data was read successfully.

Here is a snippet of code that would read 100 bytes of unformatted data from one of the files you opened previously.

```
byte Buffer[100];
fread(Buffer, 1, 100, f);
```

This will store 100 bytes of data (one byte per item * 100 items) read from the file that f points to, in Buffer, an array of 100 bytes.

Just as fread is used for reading unformatted data from a file, fwrite is used for *writing* unformatted data. The parameters for fwrite are exactly the same as fread. The first parameter is the buffer containing the data to write to the file, the second and third parameters hold the sizes of the data to be written, and the fourth is a file pointer so fwrite knows which file to output the data to. Here is code to take the data you just read in (now stored in Buffer) and write it back to the file.

```
fwrite(Buffer, 1, 100, f);
```

Sometimes you need to read or write formatted data to a file. In these cases, fread and fwrite will not work. You will need to look toward functions such as fscanf and fprintf for formatted input and output. These functions are used just like their text counterparts scanf/sscanf and printf/sprintf. Other functions are in place to read or write single variables to files such as fputc/fgetc (single characters) and fputs/fgets (strings).

All of this is very useful, but what if you need to write or read data to or from other parts of the file? You simply use the fseek() function. fseek will move your file pointer to a new place in the file. The fseek function takes three variables. The first parameter takes the file pointer you want to manipulate. The second argument takes the number of bytes you want to move, relative to the origin. The origin point is given by the third parameter. The origin can be one of three constant values:

- SEEK_BEGIN places the origin at the beginning of the file. In this case, fseek will move the specified number of bytes from the start of the file.

- SEEK_END is the second choice. SEEK_END will place the origin at the end of the file and fseek will move in reference to that location.

- The final constant for the origin is SEEK_SET. SEEK_SET will tell fseek to move the specified number of bytes from the current location in the file. After fseek is called, you may return to reading and writing your file. This time, the file is coming from or going to a new location.

When you are done reading or writing from a file, you need to close it. Failing to close a file leaves some memory allocated, thus creating a memory leak in your program. To close a file you opened with fopen, you use fclose. fclose() takes a single parameter, the file pointer of the file you want to close. You can also use the _fcloseall() to close all open files; it takes no parameters at all and returns the number of files it successfully closed. Here, you see the simple code necessary to close the file f once you are done working with it.

```
fclose(f);
```

Well, there you have it. A short introduction to file I/O using FILE *. This should be plenty to get you started loading your own 3D models. If you want to know more, or would like to learn about other methods of file I/O, I would suggest picking up a book on C or C++. Any good C/C++ book will contain a section pertaining to file I/O, whether covering FILE * or another method.

With that out of the way, and a review of file I/O complete, you are ready to move onto the hard part—deciphering the MD2 format.

Looking at the Source Code

Before you begin, you might want to pull up the source code for this chapter. The files pertaining to the MD2 models are named md2.h and md2.cpp. Both of these files can be found in the Code/Chapter_3 directory on the CD. The first thing to look at is a general layout of the file. The MD2 file contains geometry, texture, and animation information, all in a very specific order, as shown in Figure 3.2.

The first thing in every good 3D graphics file is the header. A header is simply information about the particular file located right at the start of the file. Headers are very useful because they can reveal lots of information about a file, without forcing you to dig through piles of data. Headers

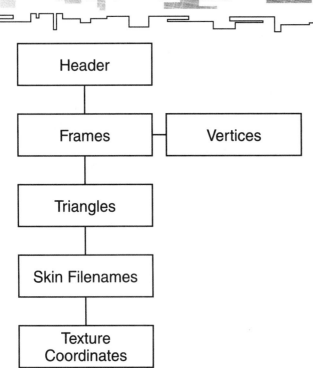

Figure 3.2 *The general layout of the data within an MD2 file.*

may include features such as "magic numbers" to identify the file type and the version numbers to prevent old file versions from being used when a program no longer contains support for it, as well as information about the data that is in the file. MD2 is no different. The header contains a plethora of useful information. Let's see what it looks like.

```
struct SMD2Header
{
        int m_iMagicNum;
        int m_iVersion;
        int m_iSkinWidthPx;
        int m_iSkinHeightPx;
        int m_iFrameSize;
        int m_iNumSkins;
      int m_iNumVertices;
      int m_iNumTexCoords;
      int m_iNumTriangles;
      int m_iNumGLCommands;
      int m_iNumFrames;
```

```
int m_iOffsetSkins;
  int m_iOffsetTexCoords;
int m_iOffsetTriangles;
int m_iOffsetFrames;
int m_iOffsetGlCommands;
int m_iFileSize;
};
```

Wow, that's a lot of information. Now that you have that list, let's see what it is all for.

- First up is the "magic number". The magic number lets you check to make sure that the file you are loading is indeed an MD2. The magic number is IDP2, which stands for ID Polygon 2. Combined into one integer, IDP2 turns out to be 844121161.

- Following the magic number is the version number. This is always 8, always. These two values should be checked upon load. If either is wrong, the file is not a valid MD2 model, and therefore will not load correctly.

- The next two variables deal with the skin, or texture, that is used to cover the model. Each MD2 can use exactly one skin at a time, although multiple skins may be loaded and used at different times (more on that in a bit). The two four-byte integers, m_iSkinWidthPx and m_iSkinHeightPx, represent the skin's height and width, respectively, in pixels.

- Always one in every family, the next variable is a bit of an odd one. m_iFrameSize, also an integer, gives you the size of each keyframe in bytes. It saves a bit of time later, but it's nothing that couldn't be easily computed later.

The next six variables are all about the numbers of things, as described:

- The first (m_iNumSkins) is the number of skins defined in the file. This variable does not refer to the number of skins used to texture the model, but rather to the total number of skin options for the model. Different skins may be used to change the appearance slightly for things such as team colors and to add a bit of variation within the game.

- m_iNumVertices, as the name implies, gives you the number of vertices per frame. Every frame in the model will contain exactly this many vertices.

- `m_iNumTexCoords` gives you the number of texture coordinates within the file. This does not need to be the same as the number of vertices. All the frames use the same set of texture coordinates.

- `m_iNumTriangles` is the number of triangles in the whole model. MD2 models contain only triangles; there are no other primitives such as quadrilaterals present.

- The next integer, `m_iNumGLCommands`, is a special one. It specifies the number of special commands that can be used to optimize the MD2's mesh into triangle fans and strips for the renderer. The GL commands are not necessary to load the model, but provide an alternative way of rendering the model.

- The last variable in this section, `m_iNumFrames`, gives you the number of frames in the MD2 file. Each frame contains a full set of vertex positions for that stage in the animation. Every frame of the model is like a snapshot of its current position.

The next section of five integers gives the offset in bytes of each of the major parts of the file, enabling you to simply skip to them when you are loading. Keep in mind that these are the distances from the beginning of the file, not the variable in the header or from the previous section of data. If you measure the distances from the wrong place, you will end up in the wrong section of the file.

The very last variable, `m_iFileSize`, gives you the file size from the start of the header, to the end of the file in bytes.

Just remember that all the integers are four bytes, giving the header a total size of 68 bytes. Now, to really get anything useful, you need to use that information along with the data structures discussed next. Read on!

The Data: Frames and Vertices

To display anything, you first need to get the data out of the file. You can start with the frames. Each frame starts with six floating-point values representing the scale and translation of the vertices on the X, Y, and Z axes. These values are used to decompress the vertices (more on this in a second). Immediately after these values comes a 16-character string that designates the frame's name. The frame name is not overly useful in the code in this book, but you may be able to find a good use for it.

Immediately following the name comes all the vertex positions for that frame. In every frame, there is exactly the number of vertices indicated by the m_iNumVerts variable in the header.

My frame structure looks like this:

```
struct SMD2Frame
{
    float m_fScale[3];
    float m_fTrans[3];
    char m_caName[16];
    SMD2Vert * m_pVertss
    SMD2Frame()
        {
            m_pVerts = 0;
        }
        ~SMD2Frame()
        {
            if(m_pVerts)
                delete [] m_pVerts;
        }
};
```

The first thing you probably notice about the structure is that it has a constructor and a destructor. This is perfectly legal in C++, and allows your frame structures to clean up after themselves so you don't have to worry about it. Another way to do it is to statically allocate an array to hold the maximum number of vertices allowed by the MD2 format (2048 vertices). However, this method wastes a considerable amount of

CAUTION

You need to be careful when working with structures, particularly ones that include pieces other than variables, such as functions, in them. The size of these structures (found with sizeof()) might not match the size of the structure in the model file. This is also true with structures such as SMd2Vertex, discussed in the next section, because the data that it stores is in a different format than is stored in the file. Be sure to watch out for situations like these.

memory if the model is small. It is best to allocate memory for each frame with the C++ keyword new.

You can't easily use the previous structure if you do not know what the vertex structure looks like. Take a look:

```
struct SMD2Vert
{
    float m_fVert[3];
};
```

That's pretty simple; m_fVert is an array of three floating-point values representing the X, Y, and Z positions of the vertex.

The vertices are not actually stored as floating point values. They are compressed into one byte for each vertex component. To decompress them, you must multiply each byte component by its respective floating-point scale value, and add the appropriate translation value. When this is done, the result can be stored in the SMD2Vert structure.

For each vertex, you read four bytes of the file into a temporary array. Following that, you multiply the first byte by the first scaling value, the second value by the second scaling factor, and so on. Then, in the same fashion, add the appropriate translations.

Once you have all this loaded, you can actually draw your model. You simply draw a single point at each vertex and you should see a rough image of the final model, similar to Figure 3.3. Not very exciting perhaps, but more than you had just a few pages ago. To really make it look good, you need to make it solid.

Making It Solid: Triangles

Triangles in MD2 files are made using vertex indexes. For each triangle, three two-byte integer values are stored, each representing a vertex in the vertex array. If the three values are 4, 6, and 14, those values can be used to index into the vertices of the current frame. All frames use the same triangle indexes when being drawn.

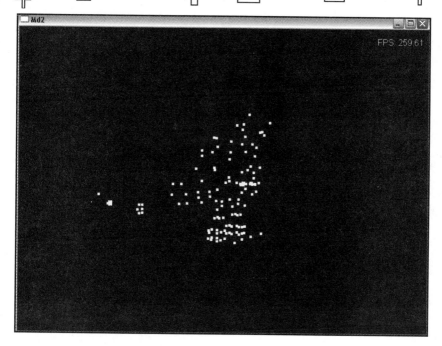

Figure 3.3 *An MD2 model with only the vertices rendered. You can see a rough outline of the model beginning to take shape.*

The triangle structure looks like this:

```
struct SMD2Tri
{
    unsigned short m_sVertIndices[3];
    unsigned short m_sTexIndices[3];
};
```

Exactly m_iNumTriangles of these structures is stored at m_uiOffsetTriangles bytes in the file.

In addition to the three vertex indexes, each triangle contains the same amount of indexes into the texture coordinate array, which you will get to in a second. Each vertex index has an accompanying index into the array of texture coordinates. This allows textures to be added easily.

Using this information, you can draw the whole model as triangles as shown in Figure 3.4. Finally, the model is starting to look decent; all it really needs are some textures.

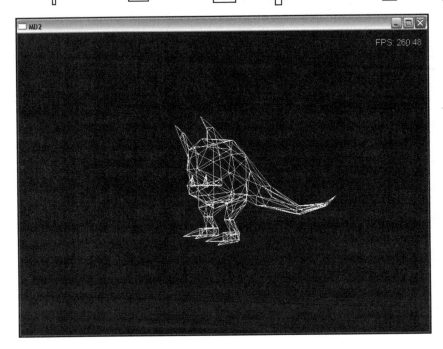

Figure 3.4   *The first render of an MD2 object, in wireframe mode.*

Rendering the Results for the First Time

I bet you are anxious to see some results of your hard work, even though you haven't added textures yet. In this section, you learn how to render the frames by themselves. A frame in the case of an MD2 model is simply a snapshot of the model in a certain position—simply different versions of the same set of vertices. For this reason, the other aspects of the model, such as the vertex indexes and texture coordinates, do not change.

It's fairly simple; all you need are a few simple OpenGL commands, as follows:

- `glBegin(GL_TRIANGLES);` tells the OpenGL that the vertices you send to it should be formed into triangles with every three vertices forming a separate triangle.

- The `glVertex3fv` command sends OpenGL an array of three floating-point values that make up a three-dimensional vertex.

- Last, glEnd() tells OpenGL that you are done rendering the triangles. All you need to do is render plain old triangles.

Take a look at the following code:

```
glBegin(GL_TRIANGLES);    //You want to render triangles
for(int i = 0; i < m_Head.m_iNumTriangles; i++)
    //Loop through all the triangles, the number of
    //which is given in the file header.
{
   //each triangle has exactly three vertices
   //the triangle structure contains three vertex indexes,
   //and each frame contains its own vertices
   glVertex3fv(
m_pFrames[frame].m_pVerts[m_pTriangles[i].m_sVertIndices[0]]);
   glVertex3fv(
m_pFrames[frame].m_pVerts[m_pTriangles[i].m_sVertIndices[1]]);
   glVertex3fv(
m_pFrames[frame].m_pVerts[m_pTriangles[i].m_sVertIndices[2]]);
}
glEnd();     //Finish up with the list of triangles
```

Ugh, those vertex calls are a little confusing; lets break them down a little bit more. Each vertex looks something like this:

```
m_pFrames[frame].m_pVerts[m_pTriangles[i].m_sVertIndices[0]]
```

- *m_pFrames* is an array that holds all of your frame data, including vertices.

- *frame* is an index into the array of frames, it tells you which set of vertices to use. For instance, if *frame* was 0, it would use the vertices from frame #0.

Because each frame has its own set of vertices, .m_pVerts is a member of each frame structure. It holds every vertex for the frame. Using the triangle indexes, you must pick out which vertex you need. That's where m_pTriangles[i].m_sVertIndices[0] comes in. m_pTriangles is the array of triangles, each which contains three vertex indexes. The *i* indicates which triangle is currently being rendered so the renderer knows which set of indexes to use. The very last part, m_sVertIndices[0], is the vertex index itself. Being that there are three of them, one for each point in the triangle, the 0, 1, and 2 are used to get each point, respectively.

Pretty cool, isn't it? To look at the complete rendering code, check out the `Render()` function of the `CMd2` class. This function will render the model in its initial position. Although there is extra code in the function for texturing, you should still be able to see the geometry code alone. Just disregard any commands with "texture" or "texcoord" in them, such as `glTexCoord2D`. The remaining code will just render the triangles; try commenting out the lines pertaining to textures and recompiling.

Beautification: Adding Skins

The model shown in Figure 3.4 would look a lot better if you added a texture. This can be done in one of two ways.

The first way is to use the skin names embedded inside the MD2 file itself. The number and location of the skin file names are dictated by variables in the header, `m_iNumSkins` and `m_iOffsetSkins`, respectively. Each skin name is 64 characters long, but the last part of the name in the file can be all zeros, effectively terminating the string at that point.

If you look at the `SMD2Skin` structure, you will notice it contains an instance of the `CImage` class. This class contains functions to load and bind various kinds of textures. There is not room to go into detail on how it works, but you are welcome to look at the source code. The files pertaining to `CImage` are in the basecode folder and are image.cpp and image.h.

Each of the file names in the skin section is a different skin. A typical skin could look something like the one shown in Figure 3.5.

Figure 3.5   *A typical skin for an MD2 model. This is the skin for the HellPig MD2 created by Psionic Design (`http://www.psionicdesign.com`).*

The other way to load a skin for the model is to use the CImage class to load a file, and then bind it to the model using the model class's SetSkin function.

But wait, before you can actually render the model, you need to load the texture coordinates from the file.

The number of texture coordinates used in the file is given by the variable m_iNumTexCoords in the header of the MD2. This many texture coordinates are stored at m_iOffsetTexCoords bytes into the file. The texture coordinate structure that will be used looks like this:

```
struct SMD2TexCoord
{
    float m_fTex[2];
};
```

Each texture coordinate consists of a pair of two-byte integers. The first texture coordinate ranges from 0 to the width of the skin, the second from 0 to the height of the skin. This will not work properly with OpenGL; you must convert them into a floating-point value between 0 and 1. To do so, you take the first short integr (two bytes), and divide it by the width of the skin, which is given by the variable m_iSkinWidthPx in the header. The same thing is done to the second coordinate, only using the number in m_iSkinHeightPx instead. This is done over and over until all the texture coordinates are calculated. Once this is done, you can move to the last step.

All that is left to do now is modify your rendering function to use the texture coordinates. First thing you do is enable texturing and bind the texture using the Bind function included in the CImage class.

Then, you travel down to the loop that draws the triangle. In the same way as the vertex indexes, the triangle structure also contains indexes into the texture coordinate array, one index for each vertex.

They work the same way, except there is only one array of texture coordinates, not one for each frame because only the positions of the vertices change between frames; the texture coordinates stay the same.

Take a look at the new rendering code:

```
glBegin(GL_TRIANGLES);     //You want to render triangles
for(int i = 0; i < m_Head.m_iNumTriangles; i++)
    //Loop through all the triangles, the number of which is
```

```
    //given in the file header.
{
    //each triangle has exactly three vertices and three texture coords
    //the triangle structure contains three vertex indexes, and each frame
    //a single array of texture coordinates is used for all of the frames
    //and they are accessed in much the same way as the vertices
    glTexCoord2fv(m_pTexCoords[m_pTriangles[i].m_sTexIndices[0]]);
    glVertex3fv(
m_pFrames[frame].m_pVerts[m_pTriangles[i].m_sVertIndices[0]]);
    glTexCoord2fv(m_pTexCoords[m_pTriangles[i].m_sTexIndices[1]]);
    glVertex3fv(m
_pFrames[frame].m_pVerts[m_pTriangles[i].m_sVertIndices[1]]);
    glTexCoord2fv(m_pTexCoords[m_pTriangles[i].m_sTexIndices[2]]);
    glVertex3fv(
m_pFrames[frame].m_pVerts[m_pTriangles[i].m_sVertIndices[2]]);
}
glEnd();        //Finish up with the list of triangles
```

That was pretty simple. Your model should look much better now, perhaps like Figure 3.6.

Figure 3.6 *A textured model. Here's the HellPig again!*

Making It Move: Animation

Now that you have a nice, textured model, you can start writing the code to animate it onscreen. Animation of a keyframed model such as an MD2 essentially involves drawing the frames one after another.

You can take the approach of simply drawing the next frame in the series, but this will produce less than satisfactory results. This method will result in jerky animation, and will run at different speeds on different computers; something you definitely do not want.

The solution to this issue is to *interpolate* between the frames with respect to time. In order to have smooth animations, you will automatically create new frames that represent the model's position at any given time. This approach has many advantages. It provides smooth transitions between frames. You can control the speed of the animation, and the frames will pass at the same rate on all machines. Last of all, it is predictable. You can count on it being at frame x during time y; even if the system gets hung up, the program will skip to wherever it should be at the time it starts again.

To do anything with time, you need a timer. The CTimer class is provided just for that, you can find out how it works by examining timer.h. The function you are most interested in here is CTimer::GetMS(). This function returns the number of milliseconds that have elapsed since the function was called.

If you know how many milliseconds have passed since the last frame, and how long each frame should last in milliseconds, you can "create" a new frame that is partway between two frames of the MD2 model.

First, you need the time it should take between frames (in ms). The Animate() function of CMd2 takes care of that. A parameter is passed to the function that tells the function how fast to animate, in frames per second. Using this it is a simple matter of obtaining the number of milliseconds for each frame. The timer takes care of the time elapsed between frames.

Using these values, you can calculate an *interpolation value.* This will let you calculate the vertices to display. Use the following formula:

$$V_0 + (V_1 - V_0)t$$

In this equation, v_0 is the vertex position of the last previous frame, v_1 is the vertex position of the next frame, and t is the interpolation value. The interpolation value must be between 0 and 1. If it isn't, it means that you have to skip frames. The next part does just that, it keeps adding one to the frame number, and decreasing the interpolation value by 1.0, until it is between 1 and 0. Once this is done, you will know what frame the value falls between. If the last frame is 19, the next frame will be 20, and if the interpolation value is 0.871, you are essentially calculating frame 19.871.

To accomplish this, you obviously need somewhere to store the inter-polated vertices. The code provided simply uses an array of CMd2Vertices with the same number of slots as each frame. This pro-vides a place to put every transformed vertex.

Next you must actually calculate the intermediate vertices. Using linear interpolation to calculate the new vertices can be done using the previous formula.

Now that you have an array of vertices, they can be rendered as a regular frame, as you did earlier in the chapter.

As you look at the code, you will notice that there are static variables that hold information such as the current frame and the last interpola-tion value. The values of these variables are stored between calls to the function, eliminating the need to store them in the class or in global variables. This function is called every time the main game or render-ing loop is executed.

One last shot of the model, in mid-animation, is shown in Figure 3.7.

Strips and Fans: GL Commands

The MD2 format also contains instructions to let you use triangle fans and strips, instead of just raw triangles. Using triangle strips and fans can help you speed up the rendering of your 3D models. The secret? Triangles share two of their vertices with another triangle, rather than having three of their own.

Say you have an object with four connected triangles. Using regular triangles, you would need a total of twelve vertex calls, three for each triangle. When using fans or strips, however, this is not the case. The first three vertices of a triangle fan or triangle strip define the first triangle in the series. Each vertex after that defines a new triangle,

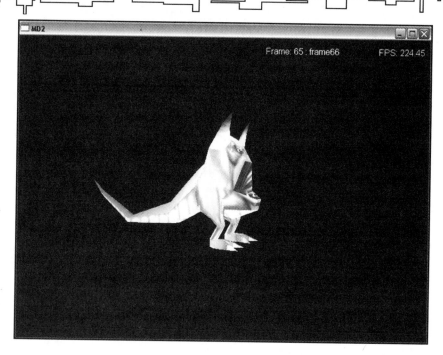

Frame: 65 : frame66   FPS: 224.45

Figure 3.7 *The model in mid-animation.*

meaning a total of only six vertices are needed. The reason for this is simple. A new triangle is formed using the new vertex, plus two of the vertices that have already been sent to the renderer.

With a triangle strip, the most recent two vertices are used in conjunction with the new vertex to create a whole triangle, creating a shape like the one shown in the center of Figure 3.8. Triangle fans work almost the same way. However, instead of using the most recent two vertices to complete the triangle, a triangle fan uses the most recent vertex and the very first vertex instead. This creates a shape like the one shown on the right side of Figure 3.8.

An MD2 model contains a set of commands; each one represents a triangle strip or fan. Each fan or strip will contain a set of vertex indexes to use in place of the normal face indexes defined earlier in the file. Each vertex index will also contain its associated texture coordinate to replace the texture coordinates loaded earlier.

At the offset designated by the header, there are a set number of GL commands (also designated by the header). Each command is exactly four bytes and can be an integer or a floating-point value.

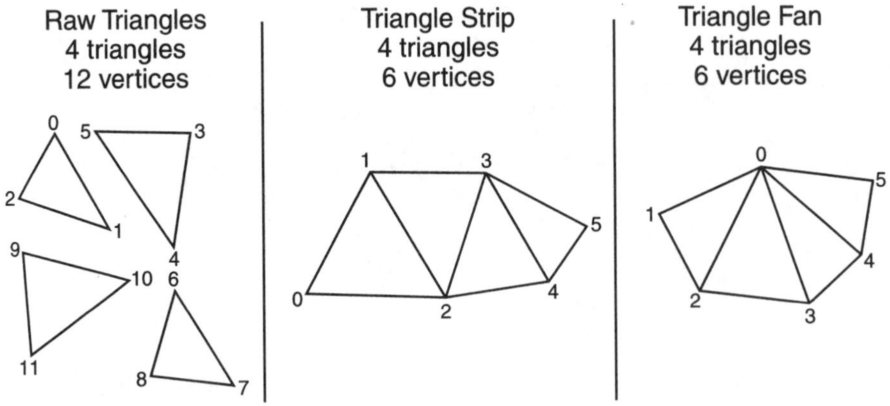

Raw Triangles
4 triangles
12 vertices

Triangle Strip
4 triangles
6 vertices

Triangle Fan
4 triangles
6 vertices

Figure 3.8   *The difference between raw triangles, triangle strips, and triangle fans.*

Each primitive starts out with an integer. This integer tells you how many vertices are in the primitive. It also tells you what type of primitive it is; if the number is negative, it is a triangle fan, positive means it is a triangle strip. The number of vertices for the fan or strip is the absolute value of that integer.

Immediately following that are the vertices. For each vertex, there are two floating-point texture coordinates ready to be plugged into the renderer without modification. Right after the two texture coordinates is an integer that is the index into the array of vertices. This pattern repeats for every vertex.

After all the vertices have been cycled through for the current primitive, you start rendering another primitive in the same way. For time and clarity's sake, I did not include code to do this, but hopefully this description should be enough to get you going.

Conclusion

Well, that concludes the chapter on the MD2 format. Using the information here, as well as the code on the CD, you should be able to write your own loader for use in your own game or demo. Have fun. If you have any suggestions, or maybe need a little bit of help, be sure to visit my site and post on the forums, or e-mail me. To find the forums, point your favorite browser to http://www.codershq.com and click the Forums link. If you prefer private email to public forums, my email address is evan@codershq.com. Also be sure to visit Psionic Designs at http://www.psionicdesign.com/. They created the HellPig model that you see in the figures of this chapter. Their model (Hellpig.Md2) is also included on the CD in the same directory as the code.

Now that you have an understanding of a simple binary format, let's move onto another type, ASCII. In the next chapter, you will learn about the OBJ format, created by Alias|Wavefront (http://www.aliaswavefront.com), for use with its popular modeling package, Maya.

CHAPTER 4

LOADING
OBJ FILES

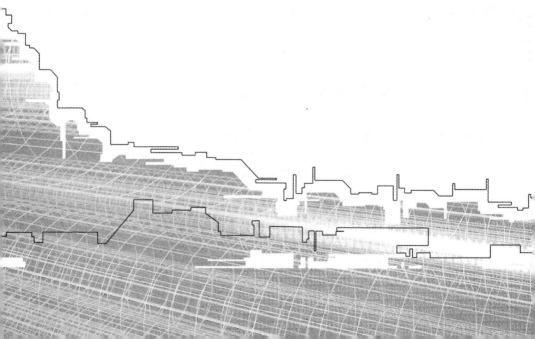

Next in line is the OBJ file format. This is a great format for static objects in a game, such as simple pieces of level geometry, weapons lying on the ground, and power-ups scattered throughout a level. The OBJ format can be exported from *Maya*, one of the industry standards for creation of 3D content, including 3D worlds and of course 3D models for games. Used by many game developers and artists worldwide, Maya has become one of the most popular 3D modeling programs around. Maya is developed and sold by Alias|Wavefront (`http://www.aliaswavefront.com`).

A simple, ASCII-based format, the OBJ model format contains geometry data, but no animation. You might want to use this format if you need to be able to edit, or even create, the files by hand, without a modeling package. This is also a great format to use if you do not need animation because it is very easy to work with. Although it can contain features such as curved surfaces, such features are beyond the scope of this book. This chapter covers just the basic geometry. This includes the faces that make up the model, along with the vertices that make up the faces themselves. It also includes texture coordinates to allow a texture map to be added, as well as vertex normals used for lighting.

Parsing Text Files

Before you can work with ASCII files, you must know how to extract the information you need, also called *parsing*, from the file.

C++ is pretty strict about what it datatypes. You can't simply set an integer equal to a string containing an integer in text format and expect it to work as you thought. Rather, you must extract and convert the data using special functions. Two of the best functions for doing this are sscanf (for extracting data from strings) and fscanf (for doing the same with files). Both functions take the same parameters, with the exception of the very first parameter. The very first parameter for sscanf is a string that holds the unformatted data, whereas the first parameter of fscanf is the file pointer you want to extract the data from.

The second parameter is the most important. It holds a string called the *format string*. The format string tells scanf which types of variables to look for and in what order they are. An example of a format string follows, and Table 4.1 shows you how to build your own format string.

The last variables are pointers to the variables you want to store your converted values in. You need a separate pointer for each value you read in. Because the scanf functions take a variable number of arguments, you can read in as many values at one time as you like.

This is best tied together with a simple example. Say you have a string, called szVertex, that contains the line:

```
Vertex 15 - [14.12, 12.51, 33.10];
```

You can see that there is a string, an integer, and three floating-point values, as well as some extra stuff such as commas, brackets, and a semicolon. You want to extract the useful parts and store them in the correct datatypes so you can use them later on in your program.

The sscanf function would look like this:

```
sscanf(szVertex, "%s %d - [%f, %f, %f];", s, &i, &f1, &f2, &f3);
```

As you can see, the format string looks a lot like the original line, only with the actual values removed. The % arguments tell sscanf what kind of variable to look for at that location. Table 4.1 shows you the most common % arguments and what they stand for. The last set of parameters lists the destination variables. s stands for a string, probably an array of characters, &i is a pointer to an integer, and &f1, &f2, and &f3 are pointers to floating-point numbers to hold the three values between the square brackets. Be sure your destination variables match up with the appropriate argument in the format string (s goes with the string, i with the integer, and f1, f2, and f3 with the three floating-point values). You can do everything shown here with fscanf, only the first parameter is the file pointer rather than a source string.

Understanding the OBJ Format

As mentioned, the OBJ format is in plain text. If you open it in Notepad or Wordpad, you'll see lists of vertices and other geometry. Having an ASCII (plain text)-based format rather than a binary one has advantages

Table 4.1   Parameters for Building a Format String

Parameter	Use
%s	A %s as a format string means that scanf will look for a string. It will read until it finds a null, space, or newline character.
%c	%c reads a single character. It will read the first character it sees, regardless of what type it is, even a space or a newline.
%d	Reading in integers uses %d. With integers scanf will read until it finds a space, letter, or symbol that is not part of a number. Integers read with %d can be positive or negative.
%f	%f is used for reading real numbers, particularly floating point values. It will cause scanf to read a number the same way as %d, but it will include decimals.

and disadvantages. Because they are stored in plain text, it is easier for a person to edit the file by hand. This can be good or bad. It is a good thing if you need to tweak small parts of the model, but these innocent tweaks can end in disaster if you accidentally change the way the file is laid out. ASCII formats also tend to take up more disk space than binary-based formats because they require extra space for large values due to their length. One "part" of the geometry is on each line.

There are four types of lines you're looking for. They are the lines that give you details about a vertex, a texture coordinate, a vertex normal, or a face. There may be other lines for things like curved surfaces and comments as well, but you will not be needing them here.

Each line of the model file starts with one or two letters that tell the program what that line is for. There are four prefixes, one for each of the important types, as described here:

- v: A letter v followed by a space is a plain vanilla vertex. If this is the case, following a single space will be three floating-point values, each separated by a single space as well.

- vt: The string vt signifies that the line contains texture coordinates. Each texture coordinate is two floats, again separated by one space.

- vn: vn signifies a vertex normal. Other than the prefix, the line mirrors the vertex lines: three floats.

- f: An f signifies a face. A face is a set of indexes into the arrays of vertices, texcoords, and normals. However, only the vertex indexes must be present; the other two are optional. Every vertex index should be positive. A negative value in the face structure probably means the file is corrupt because you cannot have a negative array index. It wouldn't be right to say "retrieve the negative second object," so you obviously could not retrieve the "negative second" vertex either. The best approach if you find a negative value within a face structure is to simply ignore the face altogether.

- Anything else: Any other line of prefixes such as g (group), # (comments), p (point), l (line), surf (surface), and curv (curve) should be ignored for now. Although they are part of the format, they are not covered here.

A typical line in the OBJ file that represents a face or triangle and contains only vertices would look something like this:

```
f  1 2 3
```

This code says that the faces use the first, second, and third vertex indexes to draw the triangles. The absence of any other sets of indexes indicates that texture coordinates and vertex normals are not needed.

If the faces are textured, but contain no vertex normals, the syntax would be similar to this:

```
f  1/4 2/5 3/6
```

This line says that the triangles use vertices 1, 2, and 3 and texture indexes 4, 5, and 6.

Yet another variation of this line could use all three types of vertex data, the vertex, texture coordinate, and normal indexes. A line that does that would look like:

```
f  1/4/7 2/5/8 3/6/9
```

The first number is for the vertex itself, the second is for its texture coordinate, and the third is for the vertex normal.

There is only one more variation: vertex and vertex normals, but no texture coordinates. It looks like this:

```
f 1//4 2//5 3//6
```

Two slashes separate the numbers instead of one; this indicates that the second number is a vertex normal, not a texture coordinate.

The fact that the faces don't need to contain all of the information can be very useful. There is no reason an object that needs no lighting or texturing should contain that information. By simply leaving the unneeded information out, the file size is reduced considerably.

Let's now move on to some code that shows you how to load the file into something you can work with.

Loading the OBJ Format

Because the OBJ does not contain any sort of header, you need some sort of resizable array to hold your vertices, faces, and the other components. In the implementation shown here, everything is loaded into an STL vector, a kind of resizable array.

Each data type has its own structure. Vector3 contains two floats and is used to hold a single vertex position, or vertex normal. Vector2 is a lot like its bigger brother, but holds only two values, perfect for texture coordinates. Last of all is SObjFace, which contains 12 unsigned integers, three for each vertex indexes, texture coord indexes, and normal indexes. Even if all the face variables are not always used, the storage is still there.

Now you are ready to read in the file. The best way to do this is read in one line at a time, check the prefix, and extract the rest of the values using the sscanf function. Each type of value (vertex data, vertex normal, texture coordinate, and face) has its own arrays to hold it. If the loader finds a line that starts with something that does not signify a recognized chunk, it simply reads the line and discards it.

In the CObj class, there are two Boolean values: m_bHasTexCoords and m_bHasNormals. These variables are set to true if a texture coord (for m_bHasTexCoords) or vertex normal line (for m_bHasNormals) is found in the file. Although this does work, it has a few flaws. If for some reason the faces do not come after all the vertex info, the loader will not know what type of face to read and will default to reading vertices only.

CAUTION

Because the OBJ format can be unpredictable and also because it can be edited easily, it is helpful to have some error checking in place. For instance, the face structures may reference invalid vertices, such as vertex number –2, or a vertex number greater than the total number of vertices. To avoid problems later, you should incorporate some error checking into your code. Every time you load a value, be sure to check if it is valid. For instance, none of the numbers on the face line should be negative. Because they are indexes into an array, they must be positive or the program may crash. The same goes for values greater than the total number of vertices, texture coordinates, or normals. If a face references a vertex outside of what it should, the best option is to ignore that face completely. Doing this will probably result in a hole in your model, but a small hole will look better than an ugly protrusion or artifact if you try to guess what the index should be.

This can cause unexpected results such as missing or deformed geometry, or even the model not showing up at all. If this happens, the easiest fix is to simply open the file and move the vertex information to the top of the file. However, for the purposes of learning and loading the most common OBJs, this should not be a problem.

When you get down to the face data, you simply take a look at the two variables and set your sscanf parameters appropriately.

Once you have all the data collected and stored, there are a few more things you should do before rendering. If you look closely at the class, you will notice that there are pointers for all of the types, as well as the resizable vectors. There is a very good reason for this.

The easiest way to access the elements of an STL vector is through the operator[] as you do with a standard array. However, this method can be quite slow and is not recommended, particularly if you need to use it each time you render a single frame, as is the case with the OBJ format.

The solution to this is to simply set the pointers to the first element in the STL vector. This does not cause a problem because STL vectors are guaranteed to be continuous. This simple technique speeds the program up a lot.

Now that all of your data is organized, you can start worrying about rendering.

Rendering OBJ

Let's see what you can do about getting this thing onscreen. If you turn to the `CObj::Render()` function in obj.cpp, you will see what it takes to get everything onscreen. The first thing to do is to activate and bind the texture. Make sure to check if the texture is valid before calling bind to avoid problems.

Then you can start rendering. The first thing that happens is it checks to see which components are included in the model and picks a loop based on the result. There is a separate loop for every possible combination to improve the speed. In pseudo-code, the rendering code would look like the following code. Keep in mind the pseudo-code gives you only a basic layout of how a function should look. It should be obvious that the following code will not compile in a regular C/C++ compiler.

```
for(each vertex)
    if(normals are present)
      SendNormal();
    if(texcoords are present)
      SendtexCoord();
    SendVertex()
```

That would require two `if` statements for every vertex, which is a waste of processor time when you can do with but a couple for every frame. Instead, the structure is more like this:

```
if(has normals and tex coords)
    for(each vertex)
      SendNormal()
      SendTexCoord()
      SendVertex()
else if(has texcoords but not normals)
    for(each vertex)
      SendTexCoords()
      SendVertex();
```

TIP

Because the geometry is static, you might want to consider compiling all of your rendering code into a display list. A display list creates a precompiled object and will drastically cut down on the processing time needed for each frame. This can be done at load time in OpenGL using the functions glGenList and glNewList. Then, in your rendering function, instead of sending every vertex to the renderer, you simply run glCallList with the appropriate display list to display your model.

And so on. Although this approach is longer, it is much more efficient. To get the appropriate values for each of the components, you use the face structure to index into the arrays of normals, tex coords, and vertices. There is one little quirk here, however. For some reason, the creators of the OBJ format decided to make 1 the first index, instead of 0. To counter this, you must subtract 1 from each of the vertex, texture coordinate, and vertex normal indexes that make up a face. This is done at load time in the demo code; see the constructor of SObjFace for more information. Have fun.

Take a quick look at the fully rendered model, shown in Figure 4.1.

TIP

The OBJ format actually has much more to offer. It can support multiple kinds of curved surfaces, faces that have more than three sides, and other cool stuff. If you are feeling ambitious, try modifying the loader to work with all of the extra stuff. There are documents of the complete OBJ all over the Internet. Just type **OBJ Format** into any search engine. A couple of good links that pop up are http://astronomy.swin.edu.au/~pbourke/geomformats/obj/ and http://www.royriggs.com/obj.html. Both contain descriptions of the OBJ file format; the first URL covers the full format, including lines, points, surfaces, and curves.

Figure 4.1 *An OBJ model of a genie lantern being rendered. This particular model included only vertices. For clarity it is rendered here in wireframe. This model was created by John Spirko (http://www.iaw.on.ca/~jspirko/galleries.htm) and was found at 3D Model World (http://www.3dmodelworld.com). Be sure to check out both sites for more free models.*

Conclusion

That wraps up the chapter. Although the basic OBJ format is fairly simple, the concepts from this chapter can be used to load other ASCII-based formats you may come across, such as ASE and ASC.

The next chapter delves into some more advanced information with an introduction to skeletal animation. In the following chapter, you will see how skeletal animation has changed the gaming world and learn about some of the games that already use it. You will also learn how skeletal animation works, and why *you* might want to use it in your next game.

CHAPTER 5

An Introduction to Skeletal Animation

C ontains skeletal animation! Revolutionary skeletal animation
system! Realistic animations! Look at almost any new 3D game's
box—these words, or some form of them, jump right out at you. It
seems that every new game uses some form of skeletal animation.

You have probably seen skeletal animation in action; games such as
Half-Life, the *Unreal Tournament* series, *Soldier of Fortune II,* and *Doom3*
all use skeletal animation in one form or another. Figure 5.1 shows
one of the first games to bring skeletal animation to the home computer, in action

Figure 5.1 *One of the first popular games to use skeletal animation was* Half-
Life. *Characters and creatures alike moved much more fluidly and realistically, thanks
to skeletal animation.The result? Scarier, cooler looking monsters such as this zombie.*

Understanding Skeletal Animation

Skeletal animation is the use of "bones" to animate a model rather than editing and moving each vertex or face manually. Each vertex is attached to a bone (or in some cases multiple bones). A bone or joint is simply a control point for a group of vertices. These are similar in concept to joints in our own bodies, such as our knee or wrist joint. When the bone moves, every vertex attached to it moves as well, as shown in Figure 5.2. Even the movement of bones themselves can cause changes to other bones. This helps the model move appropriately, because movements in one portion of the body affect other parts of the body, as in real life. Consequently, programmers are required to work with the bones to calculate the transformations for the individual vertices. Although this can be more work, the result is definitely worth it.

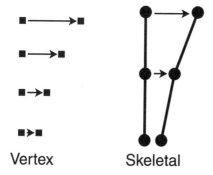

Vertex   Skeletal

Figure 5.2   *Vertex animation requires you to move every vertex, whereas skeletal animation enables you to move only the bones within the model; the vertices will follow.*

Benefits of Skeletal Animation

Skeletal animation has many advantages over the traditional vertex animation, which you saw in earlier chapters.

The first, and most visible to the game's players is increased realism. Skeletally animated characters tend to move much more realistically, and often appear to interact better with their surroundings than traditional models. The reason models tend to move more realistically if they are skeletally animated is simple. In traditional keyframe animation, the game will linearly interpolate between two poses. However, in this case, the joints do not actually rotate, which can be a problem because living organisms move in rotational ways.

Not quite as noticeable to the users, but very important to the programmers, is that such animations take up less storage space. Instead of storing a new set of vertices for each frame, all that needs to be stored is the rotation and translation of the bone. That can amount to a huge savings, even after you add the initial increased storage of the bones and vertex-bone attachment information.

This extra bit of storage space can be used to store a more detailed model, add extra animation frames, or even just be left for other parts of the game that you want to improve. You could add more detail to the game world, improve the A.I. to provide for a more exciting game, or even add some cool extras or Easter eggs that you wouldn't have added otherwise, due to space concerns.

Yet another advantage lies with the artists who create the 3D content for your games. A good skeletal animation system will cut the time the artists need to animate their models. Almost every good animation program uses skeletal animation already to ensure a smoother transition of the models from the artists to the programmer, to the game, and ultimately to the player. This speeds up the creation of content for the game, and ensures that no animations or features are lost when the models are exported into whatever format your game is using.

A fourth advantage is another one for the programmer (it just gets better and better, doesn't it?). Because of the nature of the bones, it is possible to reposition them in real-time if you want, allowing needed animations to be created during runtime. This provides a much more diverse library of possible animations. You can even let the game control the way a body acts when it collides with an object, or slides down a slope. This kind of technology is just recently coming into play, a notable example being *Unreal Tournament 2003*'s *Physics* system (http://www.epicgames.com). Characters and models react realistically with the environment, including sliding down slopes and draping over edges.

The one disadvantage is that skeletal animation can be harder to understand and implement than traditional keyframed animation. This chapter should help you alleviate any fears you might have concerning skeletal animation.

Inner Workings of Skeletal Animation

Look at your arm. Extend your limb out in front of you and take a look at it. Your arm has several bones, two main ones, and a bunch more in your hand and fingers.

Move your fingers around, just your fingers move right? By moving your fingers, no other part of your arm, or for that matter, any other part of your body moved with it. Now bend your elbow. Not only does your arm move, but your fingers and hand move up as well. If they didn't your arm would become disconnected from your hand and fingers, and they would be left hanging there in the air; not a pretty thought.

How does this little arm exercise relate to skeletal animation? Well, your arm represents part of a 3D model, your fingers, hand, lower and upper arm are all pieces of this model. Various joints and bones run through your arm, with joints at the shoulder, elbow, wrist, and fingers.

This shows you that when you move a bone "farther up" in your arm, everything below it moves as well. This is one of the most basic concepts of skeletal animation.

The beauty of this is that it allows you to move any bone in the model, and filter the movement down the line, applying it to everything below the origin of the movement. This allows you to move the shoulder of the character, for example, without needing to worry about getting the elbow and hand in the right place. You can rest assured that they will automatically be updated as well. Figure 5.3 shows a few examples of joints and vertices attached to them.

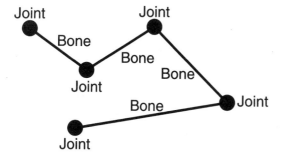

Figure 5.3 *When doing skeletal animation, you worry about the joints, or places where bones come together. Each vertex is actually attached to one of these joints, rather than to the bone itself.*

The Root Joint

The root joint is the ultimate joint in the model. Every other joint eventually finds its way back to this one joint. Any operations done on the root joint, whether they be translation or rotation, affect every vertex in the model. You can think of the root joint as the joint that controls all other joints. By simply modifying the root joint, you could make the character walk upright, or you could rotate him so he is upside down and let him walk on the ceiling—all with a single call. There is only one root joint in each model, and it has no parent joint. The root joint is generally located in a place where many bones come together, yet in a place where little animation is required. Examples of this include the middle and lower back. But there is nothing that dictates exactly where the root joint is to be located in a model; it could be different for each model if you desire. Figure 5.4 shows what would happen to a model if you modified the position and orientation of the root joint.

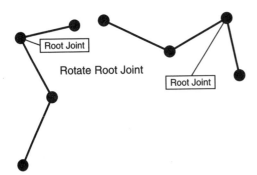

Figure 5.4   *Rotating or translating the root joint will affect all the other joints and vertices in the model.*

Parent and Child Joints

A joint can have parent and child joints. The parent of a joint affects everything it does. The parent's rotations and translations are all taken into account when computing the current joint's new position. Using the arm analogy again, the elbow joint would be the parent of the hand joint. Moving the elbow affects the hand. In simple implementations of skeletal animation, each joint has only one parent joint, if it has any at all.

However, a joint can have many child joints. A child joint is the opposite of a parent joint. Everything you do to the parent joint will filter down into the child joints. Another way to look at this is that the current joint is the parent for all of the joints below it.

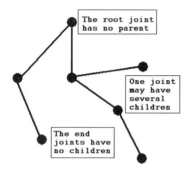

The root joint has no parent

One joint may have several children

The end joints have no children

Figure 5.5　*Parent-child joint relationships*

KeyFrames in Skeletal Animation

As with regular key-framed animation that stores multiple copies of the vertices, skeletal animation systems also have *keyframes*. Recall that keyframes are snapshots of a model's position.

However, instead of each keyframe containing its own copy of the vertices, a skeletal animation keyframe or *boneframe* contains a transformation, both rotation and translation, generally in the form of an X,Y,Z value for translation, and three values containing rotation around the X,Y, and Z axes, respectively. Just as with regular vertex keyframes, these boneframes must be interpolated to provide a smooth result.

The position or translation values can be linearly interpolated between, just as you have been doing with the vertices in traditional animation. The rotations pose a problem. Simply interpolating between them as you do with the translation values can cause strange effects. The rotation will not be smooth; it will speed up and slow down depending on its location. If the rotation differences are great, the model may appear to "ooze" like a lump of gelatin. This is because when using linear interpolation, everything gets interpolated along a straight line. This can cause strange effects when performed with rotations because rotations are meant to be interpolated along an arc rather than a line. Cutting straight across the arc rather than following it causes the "ooze" effect.

The best way to get around this is to use *quaternions*. As you learned in Chapter 2, " Introduction to Quaternions," one of the biggest advantages of quaternions is that they can be interpolated easily. Not only can they be easily interpolated; they can be easily *spherically* linearly interpolated.

Spherical linear interpolation interpolates between two points on the surface of the sphere. However, instead of cutting straight from one to the other, spherical linear interpolation follows the surface of the sphere. You can visualize this by picking up a round ball, such as a basketball, and marking two points on it. Then, using your finger, find the shortest path between the two points. Because your finger cannot go inside the ball, the resulting path between the two points will be an arc. This is what SLERP does. Using the SLERP function, the rotations can be interpolated along an arc, creating a nice smooth, eye-pleasing effect.

Taking Position

Using the information you have already read, you could try to implement skeletal animation. However, you haven't learned about how the parent joints actually affect the child joints. Simply using the keyframes would cause every joint to move independently of the rest, probably producing a strange, contorted mess.

This section talks about how to change this so that the joints work together. The first thing you do is build a transformation matrix for each point using the data from the current rotation and translation keyframes. A transformation matrix can be built by first generating the three rotation matrices and translation matrix as shown in Chapter 1. Multiplying the three together will produce a final transformation matrix. Alternatively you can use the `SetRotation` and `SetTranslation` functions in the matrix classes to avoid having to build and multiply the matrices yourself. This matrix is called the *relative matrix*.

Next, you need to calculate what is called the *absolute matrix*. The absolute matrix is the joint's relative matrix multiplied by its parent's absolute matrix. The absolute matrix tells you the joint's absolute transformation. This includes its relative transformations, as well as all of the transformations any joints before it in the hierarchy have made. This is what allows other joints to move as a result of moving a joint farther up in the line. Consider, for example, how your elbow moves when you move your shoulder. This begs the question: how do you calculate the very first absolute matrix? Keep in mind that the root joint has no parent. Therefore, its absolute matrix is the same as its relative matrix.

If you traverse down the joints in the right order, calculating the absolute matrices as you go, every joint will have its parent's transformations, and its parent's parent's transformations and so on. Figure 5.6 shows what happens when you take into account all previous transformations before transforming a joint.

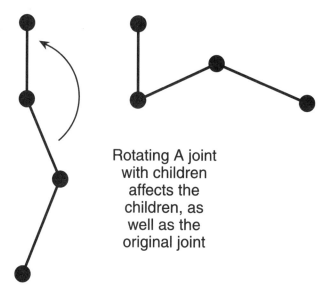

Rotating A joint
with children
affects the
children, as
well as the
original joint

Figure 5.6 *Traversing down the joints, taking into account all previous transformations. Notice that even though only one joint is told to move, the ones below it follow, much like moving your hip joint and having your knee and ankle follow as well.*

What if you do not store the joint's parent index, but rather the child indexes? This is no problem. The set of indexes you have access to right away depends on the model format. Some formats such as **MS3D** give you the parent index for each joint, whereas others give you the child indexes. Using child indexes requires a slightly different approach than using parent indexes, but is really not any harder. You start at the root joint again. After calculating the root joint's transformation matrix, you push a new matrix onto the stack with a command such as glPushMatrix. This creates a new copy of the *world matrix,* which is the matrix that all geometry is transformed by before being displayed. Now, multiply your new matrix by the root joint's local matrix.

The resulting world matrix positions everything so when the next bone is drawn, the transformation of the parent joint is taken into consideration. For example, the hip of the character may be rotated a certain amount. Because the knee and ankle joints are children of the hip joint, they will also be rotated.

The drawing function is recursive so, as each joint is drawn, it calls the drawing functions of its children. Each child calls the rendering function of its children, and so on. Only when a terminal joint is reached (one with no children), is the matrix stack reset using a command such as glPopMatrix. For example, when drawing the leg of a character, new matrices can be pushed on the stack for the knee, angle, and foot joints. But when it is time to start on the arm, you want to pop back to the original position. Otherwise, whenever you moved the leg, the arm would move as well.

Figure 5.7 shows a diagram of a recursive rendering function.

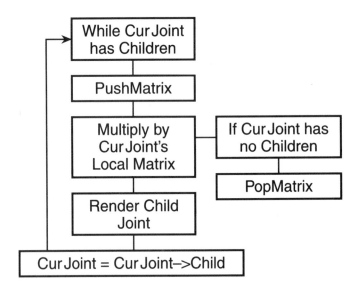

Figure 5.7   *Rendering joints that are stored with child indexes instead of parent indexes*

Attaching the Mesh

When your joints are animating smoothly, it is time to attach the mesh. The *mesh* is what makes up the shape of the model. It is a group of vertices and triangles that help the model have volume and detail. Without the mesh, a skeletally animated model would simply be a skeleton. Each mesh vertex stores an index into the joint array to signify that it is attached to a certain bone. Now, the way the joints were stored determines the method of transforming and rendering these vertices.

If the joints are stored with each having its parent index, and you have already gone through and calculated the final absolute matrices, attaching the mesh is simple. Each vertex must be transformed by its joint's absolute matrix. Be sure to store your transformed vertex in a special place; do not overwrite your original vertex. This is done because in most formats, the boneframes are not cumulative. Each frame stores the rotation and translation of a specific joint from the starting point. If you do not go back to the original vertices when calculating new vertex positions each time, the model will behave erratically. Figure 5.8 shows what it means to attach individual vertices to a joint.

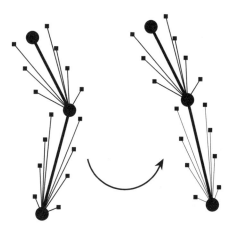

Figure 5.8 *Attaching vertices to joints.*

Now you are probably thinking to yourself, "well, I can animate a model's vertices, but what about triangles, normals, and texture coordinates"? This is where skeletal animation really starts to shine. Each model contains just one set of texture coordinates and triangle information. Just because the positions of the vertices change does not mean the triangle indexes and texture coordinates have to. This means you don't have to worry about them once you set them up.

Normals are another story. Because the orientation of the polygons and vertices change, so will the normals. If you are using just face normals, you need to recalculate them manually every frame before sending them to the renderer. However, if you calculated vertex normals at the beginning, you are in luck. Vertex normals do not have to be completely recalculated after transformation. They can be transformed by the same matrix as the vertices were. The only difference here is that you do not take in account translation. Using the Transform3() function of the matrix class will rotate your vertex normal, while still retaining its original magnitude.

If the joints store child indexes and you are pushing the current transformation matrix onto the stack using glPushMatrix, rendering your model becomes really easy. In this case, it is not necessary to transform each vertex before displaying it. No changes are necessary for rendering anything. Everything you render now will be transformed properly, even face normals. Another issue to consider is how vertices are attached to more than one bone. In this case, each bone will have an assigned weight that tells you how much it will affect the joint. The final transformation is the weighted average of all of the transformations of the attached bones.

The Demo

This chapter's demo allows you to see the relationship between parent and child joints, and see what happens when an individual joint is manipulated, as shown in Figure 5.9.

The demo allows you to pick from one of four joints and modify its rotation and translation values. These new values in turn affect joints that are farther down the line (child joints). By manipulating the different joints, you can see the effect of your actions on all the other joints.

The joint numbers are, from top of the screen to bottom, as follows: 1, 0, 2, 3. Joint 1 and 3 are terminal joints. They are right at the ends of the "model" and moving either of them will have no effect on the other joints in the model.

Joint 2 is the parent of joint 3. Changing the values of this joint causes joint 3 to move as well: try it and see. Finally, joint 0 is the root joint. Anything you do to this joint will effect every other joint on screen.

The Demo's Controls

On the left side of the screen, you will see a dialog box containing various controls and text boxes, as shown in Figure 5.10.

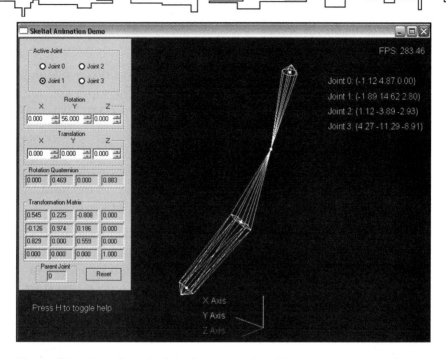

Figure 5.9   *A small simple skeletal animation demo. You can rotate and translate individual joints, using the control panel at the left, and see their effects on other joints.*

Figure 5.10   *The control panel enables you to control the position and rotation of each of the joints. Selecting the joint from the buttons on the top of the control box, and then using the up and down arrows on the control boxes enables you to translate and rotate joints in the model.*

The radio buttons on the topmost section of the control dialog box select the joint you would like to modify.

Underneath the radio buttons are six edit boxes. These boxes enable you to change the orientation of the selected joint. The top set of boxes change the joint's rotation around the X, Y, and Z axes, whereas the bottom set changes the object's X, Y, and Z translation.

Underneath those boxes is a set of read-only edit boxes. These boxes contain the equivalent rotation quaternion and transformation matrix that would be used to transform any vertices connected to the joint. A small box labeled Parent Joint displays the current joint's parent.

This demo was a lot of fun to write and can be entertaining to play with. Watch carefully to see how your actions affect the other joints in the scene. Be sure to check out the onscreen help when you first run the program. The help will be displayed onscreen when you first start and can be toggled on and off by pressing H.

TIP

Although you can translate joints in skeletal animation, it is generally best to stick with rotations. If you think about it, on your own body, none of your joints ever changes position, a higher-up joint simply rotates. For instance, if you move your hand away from your body, you do not translate the hand, you rotate the elbow instead. The human body does not have any telescoping appendages, thus almost 100% of movements can be done in terms of rotation, rather than translation.

The only exception to this guideline is the root joint. Translating the root joint will move the whole model, which is useful if you want to change the actual position of the model within the animation. You would use this if you needed your model to change position during the animation, such as to walk forward. However, it is generally best to let the game take care of moving the model around the world. This means that all models that need walk or run animations will be walking and running "in place". The game will add in the forward or backward movement later.

Advanced Applications of Skeletal Animation

That pretty much wraps up the introduction to skeletal animation. But before you go, take a look at some of cool stuff that can be done with more advanced techniques, beyond the scope of this book.

Figure 5.11 shows a shot of Epic's *Unreal Tournament 2003*. *Unreal Tournament 2003* is one of the first games to implement a good "ragdoll" system. In a ragdoll system, bodies change according to their environment. For instance, when a person is killed in the game while standing on a hill, their body does not remain lying in a straight line like is common in many other shooter games. Instead, the body slides down the hill in a realistic manner, bouncing and sliding while following the orientation of the terrain. This method of animation adds a lot to the realism and believability of any game.

Figure 5.11   *Unreal Tournament 2003's ragdoll system in action. Notice how the body drapes itself around the hole, much like a real human would.*

Conclusion

This concludes your introduction to skeletal animation. Hopefully you have a grasp of how skeletal animation works and why many games are starting to use it.

The next few chapters will use this information as you start learning about formats that use skeletal animation for animation. You will be able to see firsthand the smooth, fluid motion of models and start to appreciate the idea behind skeletal animation.

The next chapter covers the MilkShape 3D format, also known as MS3D. It is created by a shareware editor, also called MilkShape 3D. Released by its author as shareware, it is rapidly becoming one of the hottest tools for independent game developers everywhere. Its low price, the capability to output models for many different games and programs, and its expandability through plug-ins have quickly made it a favorite among artists and programmers alike. Read on to learn about this exciting and useful format.

CHAPTER 6

MilkShape 3D

A s the book moves forward into this chapter, more advanced formats start appearing. This is the first of several more complicated formats. Gone are the days of simple "load-and-cycle" formats such as the famous MD2 format discussed earlier in the book.

This chapter contains everything you need to know about the MS3D format outputted by a very nice, very inexpensive modeling package known as MilkShape 3D. MilkShape 3D was created by chUmbaLum sOft, a small software company consisting of the founder, Mete Ciragan. Mete created MilkShape to allow individuals to create new models for VALVe Software's *Half-Life* (`http://www.valvesoftware.com`) without the use of expensive professional modeling tools.

Since its creation, MilkShape has become one of the most popular modeling tools among independent developers of "mods"—smaller games built on top of commercial ones—and games alike. It now supports importing and exporting formats for many popular games and engines. I recommend that any game developer on a short budget take a look at this wonderful program. You can check out a 30-day trial on the CD. You can find the setup file in the `Programs` directory.

For your viewing pleasure, Figure 6.1 shows the MilkShape 3D editor with the model you'll be using as an example in the upcoming pages.

Getting the Data

As always, you start by getting the data out of the file. Unlike most model formats, MS3D does not contain information about the number of vertices, triangles, or anything else at the start of the file. All that is present is a simple header to verify that the file is indeed a valid MilkShape file.

The header is exactly 14 bytes long and contains a 10-character identification string, and a version number. The first 10 bytes contain the string "`MS3D000000`". This string identifies the file as a MilkShape file.

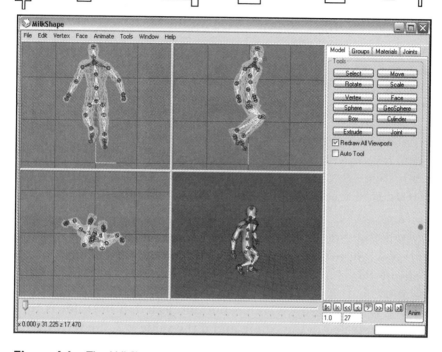

Figure 6.1 *The MilkShape 3D editor complete with an example model.*

Keep in mind that the zeroes in the ID string are characters, not values. Make sure you keep that in mind loading the file. The second four bytes contain a single integer. This is the version number of the file and should contain the value 3 or 4. The format detailed here is for these two versions only. As MilkShape progresses and new versions of the format are released, I will post additions and changes on the book's Web site.

Vertices

Directly after the header come the vertices. As with other parts of the file, the vertex chunk is prefixed by a two-byte unsigned integer that contains the number of vertices present in the model.

The vertices are a little bit different than what you have been using previously. Instead of simply an X, Y, Z coordinate plane, MilkShape's vertices also contain a one byte, signed integer that holds the number of that vertex's "bone". A value of –1 means that the vertex has no bone attached to it and is not affected during animation.

Here is the vertex structure that is used for the MS3D loader:

```
//------------------------------------------------
//- SMs3dVertex
//- A single vertex
struct SMs3dVertex
{
    unsigned char m_ucFlags;  //Editor flags, unused for the loader
    CVector3 m_vVert;         //X,Y,Z coordinates
    char m_cBone;             //Bone ID (-1 = no bone)
    unsigned char m_ucUnused;
};
```

The middle two variables in the structure were explained previously, which leaves only two one-byte variables left unknown. The first contains various flags for the editor to use for the vertex. This variable is an unsigned char that holds the status of the vertex within the editor. If the value is 0, the vertex is visible, but unselected. If the value is 1, the vertex is selected in the editor, and if the value is 2, the vertex is hidden from view in the editor window. A value of 3 means the vertex is both hidden and selected. Although this variable is not necessary for loading the models into your engine, it may be helpful if you are writing an importer for another modeling program, such as 3D Studio Max (www.discreet.com) or Maya (www.aliaswavefront.com). The second variable contains nothing; you can just skip over it.

After the vertices are read, the file moves immediately on to the face information.

Faces

The face for this particular model format contains a lot of information. But, before you worry about loading the triangles, you need to find out how many of them there are. As with the vertex chunk, the face or triangle chunk starts with a two-byte integer. This integer comes immediately after the last vertex is read, and just before the triangle data is stored. This two-byte integer contains the number of SMs3dTriangle structures to read from the file.

Right after the two-bytes worth of data that determine the number of faces to read come the faces themselves. The face or triangle structure contains editor flags, vertex indexes, texture coordinates, grouping info, and even the vertex normal information. Lets take a look at the SMs3dTriangle structure to see what solidifying the model entails:

```
//-------------------------------------------------
//- SMs3dTriangle
//- Triangle data structure
struct SMs3dTriangle
{
    unsigned short m_usFlags;              //Editor flags
    unsigned short m_usVertIndices[3];     //Vertex indexes
    CVector3 m_vNormals[3];                //Vertex normals;
    float m_fTexCoords[2][3];              //Texture coordinates
    unsigned char m_ucSmoothing;           //Smoothing group
    unsigned char m_ucGroup;               //Group index
};
```

Well, that's not too bad. A total of six variables are used for every triangle in the MilkShape 3D model. The first, like the vertex structure, is just an editor flag. Like vertices, a 0 means a regular, unselected face, a 1 means the face is selected, and a 2 means the face is hidden from view. Again, a face can be both selected and hidden if the value is 3. Notice that this flag variable here is two bytes, rather than just 1 like it is in the vertex structure.

Next come three more unsigned two-byte integers. These three integers are indexes into the array of vertices covered in the last section. The three vertices form a single triangle in the model. Using only the data covered so far, it is possible to create a solid model. However, it would be kind of boring with no textures or lighting.

Moving on down the line, you come to the vertex normals. A vertex normal is used for lighting. Each vertex normal is an average of all the normals of the faces its vertex shares. A face normal is perpendicular to the plane the face lies in; the vertex normal is the average of all the perpendicular vectors. A normal, whether it is a vertex or face normal, must be a unit vector with a magnitude of 1. These are stored in a CVector3 class. The CVector3 is made for vectors that consist of three floating-point variables that take up a total of 12 bytes. The main advantage of using a Cvector3 for each normal rather than a simple array of floats is that the CVector3 class contains a myriad of functions. These functions make it a lot easier for you later on when you start animating the model. There are three normals—one for each vertex index.

Up next are the texture coordinates. The u and v coordinates are stored kind of strangely in MilkShape. There are a total of six floats—one pair of coordinates for each of the three vertices that make up the face. However, instead of being stored u1, v1, u2, v2, u3, v3 like you might expect, MilkShape stores all the *us* first, followed by all the *vs*. This makes the order u1, u2, u3, v1, v2, and v3. If you do not remember this ordering, it will come back to bite you. I spent several hours debugging a program only to find I used the wrong texture coordinates in the wrong places.

The last two variables deal with the group the face belongs to. These variables are not too important as you will see in the section coming up. The groups or meshes in the model take care of knowing which faces belong to each group.

Meshes

For maximum flexibility, MilkShape 3D's triangles are grouped into meshes or groups. This allows different sections of the model to use different textures, materials, and even render only certain sections of the model. The mesh section of the file follows the triangle or face section, and like the other section is preceded by a two-byte integer telling how many meshes there are. Immediately following are the groups. There are 35 bytes of general information, followed by a number of two-byte triangle indexes. The number of indexes is not constant; some groups may have more than others. To compensate for this discrepancy, you need to be able to dynamically allocate memory in each group to hold these indexes. Here is what the structure looks like.

```
//-------------------------------------------------------------
//- SMs3dMesh
//- Group of triangles in the ms3d file
struct SMs3dMesh
{
    unsigned char m_ucFlags;    //Editor flags again
    char m_cName[32];           //Name of the mesh
    unsigned short m_usNumTris;//Number of triangles in the group
    unsigned short * m_uspIndices; //Triangle indexes
    char m_cMaterial;        //Material index, -1 = no material

    //Let it clean up after itself like usual
```

```
SMs3dMesh()
{
    m_uspIndices = 0;
}
~SMs3dMesh()
{
    if(m_uspIndices)
    {
        delete [] m_uspIndices;
        m_uspIndices = 0;
    }
}
};
```

This structure takes a bit of care when being read in. The m_uspIndices variable is a pointer, meaning you just can't read in NumberOfMeshes * sizeof(SMs3dMesh). For each mesh, you must read the first 35 bytes that consist of some editor flags—the same flags that the vertices and triangles use—0 for unselected, 1 for selected, and 2 for hidden. You must also read a 32-character mesh name and a two-byte integer that contains the number of triangles in the mesh. Using this last variable, you must allocate the memory for the triangles indexes.

The m_uspVariable is now ready to hold all of the two-byte integers necessary to show which triangles are used in the mesh. Each element of the array is an index into the array of triangles that was created and filled earlier in the load sequence.

Right after you read all the triangle indexes, there is a lone, single-byte variable that holds the index into the materials array (which you will be getting to in a second). The variable is signed, and a value of −1 means the mesh contains no material.

Last of all, as you can see, the structure takes care of deleting its own memory, meaning you do not have to worry about remembering to clear it when you are done using it. Deleting the array of meshes will automatically delete everything in them.

Materials

To really make the model stand out and to add lots of customization, you can use materials. Materials control the way the renderer handles the texturing and lighting of the model. From textures, to color, to transparency, materials do it all.

The materials structure is fairly large and contains a lot of data, so bear with me here.

Remember to read in your two-byte variable that tells you how many materials there are before you jump into reading the material data.

Here is the material structure:

```
//----------------------------------------------------
//- SMs3dMaterial
//- Material information for the mesh
struct SMs3dMaterial
{
    char m_cName[32];          //Material name
    float m_fAmbient[4];       //Ambient values
    float m_fDiffuse[4];       //Diffuse values
    float m_fSpecular[4];      //Specular values
    float m_fEmissive[4];      //Emissive values
    float m_fShininess;        //0 - 128
    float m_fTransparency;     //0 - 1
    char m_cMode;              //unused
    char m_cTexture[128];      //Texture map file
    char m_cAlpha[128];        //Alpha map file
    CImage m_Texture;
};
```

You need to be careful when you start reading the data from the file. Instead of reading the whole group of materials in at once, you must loop and read them in one at a time. The reason for this is the very last variable in the structure, m_Texture. m_Texture is an image class that is used to store the texture for the material. This eliminates trying to sort out the textures later when you need to use them during the program. Note that this part of the structure is not actually contained within the file, making the actual size of the structure in the file 361 bytes. The CImage variable is a custom class that resides in the general basecode in the files (image.cpp and image.h). You can easily remove this variable and replace it with your own image-loading system.

The first variable in the structure is a 32-character array that holds the name of the material. This isn't all that important if you are just making a loader, but it's nice to have when working with the model in MilkShape itself.

The next six variables contain the materials properties. These properties determine the way the lighting of the scene will affect the model.

- The m_fAmbient and m_fDiffuse each store four floating-point values that represent the red, green, blue, and alpha (RGBA) values of a color. These colors help define the color of the material and determine how the polygons using this material will react to lighting in the scene.

- The next variable, m_fSpecular, also contains an RGBA color. The specular material properties dictate the color of the specular highlights or "shiny places" on the mesh using the material.

- The last array of floats is the m_fEmissive set. This variable also contains four floats. The emissive property specifies how intense the material will emit light. The higher the values, the "brighter" the material will be.

- The final material property is the shininess of the material. The m_fShininess variable contains a single float. This variable determines just how shiny the specular highlights are. The lower the value, the darker and duller the highlights will be—just the opposite as the value increases. Darker and duller highlights are used for materials such as wood and asphalt, whereas brighter, shinier highlights are best for shiny metal and artificial materials.

After all these material properties comes one more—the transparency of the material, which is stored in m_fTransparency. Although the other material variables deal with color, transparency sets how opaque or "see-through" the mesh is. A value of 1 is completely opaque and a value of 0 is complitely transparent, or invisible. Because of the way OpenGL handles materials, the easiest way to handle this is to take this value and plug it into the last element of the diffuse property. This method creates a reasonably nice transparent mesh.

After these are all taken care of, you must skip a byte to compensate for a small, unused variable in the material information. This single byte variable m_ucMode is unused by the format for now. It is in there for use in later versions.

Then you get to the textures. The texture name is stored in a 128-byte string. After you acquire it, you can send it directly to the Load function of the `CImage` class included in the structure. This will retrieve the texture and take care of loading it so it is ready to use when you get to the rendering stage. The filename stored in the file can be passed directly to the `CImage::Load()` function or to your own texture-loading functions.

The last variable holds the filename of the alpha map. Due to the fact that I could find no information on this at the time this was written, the use of alpha maps on models is not currently supported. However, keep checking the Web site for the book and as soon as information is available I will update the code and the text and post it there.

Whew, that was a lot of information. However, you now have enough to render the model in what I call its "initial position". This is the position before any animation is applied. In general, this position is optimized for ease of editing and probably does not appear in the actual animation sequence.

Figure 6.2 shows what the model would look like rendered.

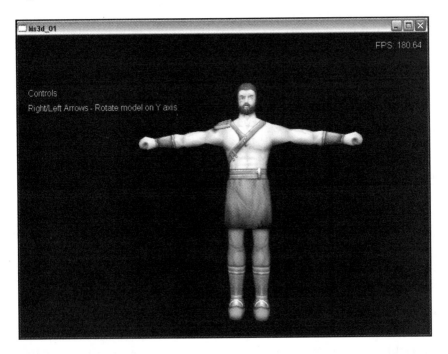

Figure 6.2 *The model rendered in its initial position with textures, materials, and lighting enabled.*

Pretty cool huh? Rendering the model isn't too hard. It basically involves drawing the meshes one by one, making sure to set the appropriate material and lighting properties beforehand. As usual, in order to make the code easier to read and convert to other languages and APIs, I use immediate mode calls that are pretty obvious in what they do.

The first thing that must be done is the material information. In OpenGL this can be done using the glMaterialf and glMaterialfv calls.

```
for(int x = 0; x < m_usNumMeshes; x++)
{
    //Set up materials
    if(m_pMeshes[x].m_cMaterial >= 0)
    {
        SMs3dMaterial * pCurMat = &m_pMaterials[m_pMeshes[x].m_cMaterial];
        //Set the alpha for transparency
        pCurMat->m_fDiffuse[3] = pCurMat->m_fTransparency;

        glMaterialfv(GL_FRONT_AND_BACK, GL_AMBIENT, pCurMat->m_fAmbient);
        glMaterialfv(GL_FRONT_AND_BACK, GL_DIFFUSE, pCurMat->m_fDiffuse);
        glMaterialfv(GL_FRONT_AND_BACK, GL_SPECULAR, pCurMat->m_fSpecular);
        glMaterialfv(GL_FRONT_AND_BACK, GL_EMISSION, pCurMat->m_fEmissive);
        glMaterialf(GL_FRONT_AND_BACK, GL_SHININESS, pCurMat->m_fShininess);
        glEnable(GL_BLEND);
        glBlendFunc(GL_SRC_ALPHA, GL_ONE_MINUS_SRC_ALPHA);

        //Texture map
        pCurMat->m_Texture.Bind();
    }
    else
        glDisable(GL_BLEND);
```

This little bit of code should be easy to follow. Because each model is broken into meshes, you must loop through them and draw them one at a time. The first thing to do is check to see whether the mesh does indeed have a material attached to it. If the material index of the mesh is not −1, a pointer to the appropriate material is obtained. Now you are almost ready to send the material information to OpenGL; however, you first must take care of transparency. This is done by taking the transparency variable and using it to replace the alpha value of the diffuse property. Once that simple operation is completed, you can set the material properties. Every property except Shininess uses glMaterialfv. This is because all other values are arrays of values, whereas shininess is simply a single float.

The next section simply turns on blending and sets the appropriate blending mode. This assures that transparency will work correctly and will minimize any funny visual artifacts.

Last, using the CImage class that you used to load the skin earlier, you bind the texture to the mesh.

If there is no material for the group, you must make sure to turn off blending. Failure to do so can cause very strange visual artifacts and unwanted graphical glitches. You can also use glMaterial to set the materials back to default. The default values for ambient, diffuse, specular, emissive materials are (0.2, 0.2, 0.2, 1.0), (0.8,0.8,0.8,1.0), (0.0,0.0,0.0,1.0), and (0.0,0.0,0.0,1.0), respectively. The shininess material is also set to 0.

The code that sends the vertices to the rendering system follows:

```
//Draw mesh
glBegin(GL_TRIANGLES);
for(int y = 0; y < m_pMeshes[x].m_usNumTris; y++)
{
    //Get a pointer to the current triangle
    SMs3dTriangle * pCurTri = &m_pTriangles[m_pMeshes[x].m_uspIndices[y]];
    //Send the normal
    glNormal3fv(pCurTri->m_vNormals[0].Get());
    //Send texture coords
    glTexCoord2f(pCurTri->m_fTexCoords[0][0], pCurTri->m_fTexCoords[1][0]);
    //Send vertex position
    glVertex3fv(m_pVertices[pCurTri->m_usVertIndices[0]].m_vVert.Get());

    glNormal3fv(pCurTri->m_vNormals[1].Get());
    glTexCoord2f(pCurTri->m_fTexCoords[0][1], pCurTri->m_fTexCoords[1][1]);
    glVertex3fv(m_pVertices[pCurTri->m_usVertIndices[1]].m_vVert.Get());

    glNormal3fv(pCurTri->m_vNormals[2].Get());
    glTexCoord2f(pCurTri->m_fTexCoords[0][2], pCurTri->m_fTexCoords[1][2]);
    glVertex3fv(m_pVertices[pCurTri->m_usVertIndices[2]].m_vVert.Get());
}
```

```
    glEnd();
  }
}
```

Just as you loop through each mesh, you must loop through each triangle within the mesh itself. After acquiring a pointer to the appropriate triangle structure in the face array, you can send the normal vector, texture coordinates, and vertex position to OpenGL. This must be done three times for each triangle and once for each vertex.

Animation

This is the part you have all been waiting for. The first section that uses what you learned in Chapter 5, "Introduction to Skeletal Animation" (you did read that didn't you?)

First thing you have to do is finish loading the model. The remaining part of the model contains the joint (bone) data, including their names, initial positions, and keyframes.

Like the other section of the ms3d file, the joints structure is preceded by a two-byte integer that tells how many joints the file contains. Then comes the data. The joints and accompanying structures are fairly complicated, so bear with me.

First, the simple structure. This structure is used for storing the rotation and translation of the keyframes:

```
//--------------------------------------------------------
//- SMs3dKeyFrame
//- Rotation/Translation information for joints
struct SMs3dKeyFrame
{
    float m_fTime;
    float m_fParam[3];
};
```

This is a simple enough structure. The keyframe structure stores a single "stop point" or landmark of the model. The first variable, fTime, stores the time in seconds that this keyframe would be used to set the position of the particular joint. The second variable is an array of three floats. They store the rotations around the X, Y, and Z axes, or they contain the X, Y, and Z translation values. Each joint contains a set of these keyframes for both rotation and translation values.

Now, on to the joint structure. This is a fairly large structure that contains a lot of data. Some of it is to be loaded from the file; some of it is created from these values instead of being loaded directly from the file.

Here again, the structure in the code varies from the structure in the file. The file contains the editor flags, the joint name, the parent joint's name, the initial position and rotation, the number of keyframes for rotation and translation, and the actual translation and rotation keyframes. As was the case back in the group structures when you needed to use a dynamically allocated array to hold the indexes, you need to allocate memory for the keyframes before reading them in.

Brace yourself. Here is the code for SMs3dJoint, the joint structure.

```
//-------------------------------------------------
//- SMs3dJoint
//- Bone Joints for animation
struct SMs3dJoint
{
    //Data from file
    unsigned char m_ucpFlags;           //Editor flags
    char m_cName[32];                   //Bone name
        char m_cParent[32];             //Parent name
        float m_fRotation[3];           //Starting rotation
        float m_fPosition[3];           //Starting position
    unsigned short m_usNumRotFrames;    //Number of rotation frames
        unsigned short m_usNumTransFrames;  //Number of translation frames

        SMs3dKeyFrame * m_RotKeyFrames;     //Rotation keyframes
        SMs3dKeyFrame * m_TransKeyFrames;   //Translation keyframes

    //Data not loaded from file
    short m_sParent;                    //Parent joint index

    CMatrix4X4 m_matLocal;
    CMatrix4X4 m_matAbs;
    CMatrix4X4 m_matFinal;

    unsigned short m_usCurRotFrame;
```

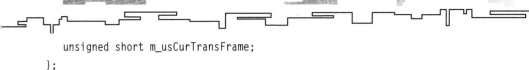

```
    unsigned short m_usCurTransFrame;
};
```

Let's walk through this step by step. Like all the data structures from MS3D, this one has one byte's worth of editor flags that can be ignored. Following that there are two 32-character strings. These strings hold the joint's name and the joint's parent's name. Later, you'll match each joint to its parent so you don't have to compare all the strings every time the joint positions need to be recomputed.

Next come the initial rotations and translations of the joints. These six values—three for rotation and three for translation—give the starting positions of the joints.

Then come two two-byte integers, one for the number of rotation keyframes and one for the number of translation keyframes. These are used to allocate memory for the next two variables that hold the actual rotation and translation data, respectively.

After allocating the memory, you can read the data from the file into the newly created arrays. This is all the data that needs to come from the file. You can close the file and get rid of any temporary buffers you may have created or allocated.

Finding the Lost Parents

Each joint stores the name of its parent. Although this name can be used, it is a pain to run lots of string compare operations and search through every joint to find the right one. It is better that this comparison be performed only once, during the loading of the model. That's where the m_sParent variable comes in. This variable is an index into the array of joints. At this index is the current joint's parent. If the joint is a root joint, meaning it has no parent, this is set to −1 to avoid confusion.

To calculate this variable for the current joint, you start at the beginning of the array and loop through the joints until one of the joint's names matches the current joint's parent's name. Be sure to determine whether the parent name is blank first. A blank parent name signifies that the joint has no parent, and it would be a waste of time to search for one.

Initial Setup

Before you can start animating, you must do a bit more setup. Each joint's matrices must be set to the initial rotation and translation, and the vertices and normals attached to each bone must be transformed by these matrices. Take a look at the CMs3d::Setup() function. (Because the function is too large to display here, you might want to refer to the code. CMs3d::Setup can be found in the Code/Chapter6 directory in ms3d.cpp. The function starts around line 490.)

The Setup function consists of three parts. The first part loops through the joints and creates the matrices. The first matrix created is the relative matrix, stored in the variable m_matLocal. This is the rotation and translation of the joint by itself. Using the m_fRotation and m_fTranslation arrays in the joint, the m_matLocal matrix can be created with the SetRotation and SetTranslation member functions of the matrix class.

Next comes the absolute matrix. The absolute matrix is simply the relative matrix (m_matLocal) multiplied by the joint's parent's relative matrix. The resulting matrix is stored in the m_matAbs variable. If the joint has no parent, the absolute matrix is the same as the relative or local matrix.

The third matrix variable (m_matFinal) is the final transformation matrix used during animation. For now, it can just be set to the same value as the absolute matrix.

The second part of the setup function involves transforming the vertices into what I call the "initial animation position". The initial animation position is simply the position assumed by the model when the joints are set using the staring rotations and translation values—the m_fRotation and m_fTranslation values—for each joint. This position might not be included in the first animation.

To perform this transformation, all you need to do is retrieve the final matrix from the joint the current vertex is attached to. The vertex must be transformed by the inverse of this matrix. The inverse of a rotation matrix will rotate the opposite way of the initial matrix. This can be accomplished using the InvRotateVec and InvTranslateVec functions included in the matrix class (matrix.inl).

Last of all, you must set the normals up to ensure proper lighting. Because the normals are stored in the face structure, you have to loop through the faces instead of the vertices. To obtain the appropriate matrix for transforming the normals, you must use the vertex indexes of the face structure to retrieve the joint and matrix used to transform the vertex, which the normal belongs to. Once you have this matrix, the normal can be rotated. Like the vertices, you use the InvRotateVec function. However, because lighting normals are unit vectors, there is no need to translate them as well.

Now, everything is set up and ready to animate.

Animation and Interpolation

Finally you get to the good stuff. All the vertices are in the right starting places, all the joints are set up, and all the other data is loaded and taken care of. Now you can animate the model.

The Animate function of the CMs3d class takes four parameters. The first is the speed. The speed is a floating-point value that designates how fast the model should animate. A value of 1.0f means the model should animate exactly as fast as it was meant to when it was created. A value of 2.0f will animate twice as fast as the original, and 0.5f will animate the model half as fast as the original and so on.

The next two parameters, fStartTime and fEndTime, tell the function which parts of the animation to use. Because each joint can have a varying number of keyframes and the keyframes of a joint do not need to occur at the same time intervals, it is unpractical to use a start and end keyframe. The fStartTime and fEndTime give a starting and ending time of the animation segment. If fStartTime is 0.3f and fEndTime is 0.9f, only the six tenths of a second worth of animation between the two times is drawn. Because there is nothing in the MS3D file that tells you where separate animations start and stop, you might record the start and end time of certain animations. For example, 0.0 to 0.5 seconds contains a run animation and 0.5 to 1.3 contains a jump animation. By plugging these values into the Animate() function, you can display just the run or just the jump animation.

Now you need to determine just what part of the animation to display at the current instant. It is not enough to just pick the keyframe with the time closest to the current time. Doing this would result in jerky, unnatural motion because the distance between keyframes can be large and the time it takes to move from one to another can be fairly long. A keyframe might exist only at the start and the end of the leg movement, and simply alternating between the two frames to represent walking would look awful. Instead, you need to interpolate between the keyframes.

Using the timer class included with the CMs3d class, you get the time that has elapsed in seconds since the last frame. Adding this time to the time elapsed since the last time the animation was restarted, and adding the result to the beginning time specified in the parameters of the function should give you a time value to use when finding the position of the model.

Armed with this time value, you can find the "current" and "previous" frame for each frame. The time value you calculated in the previous step must fall somewhere between the previous and current keyframe, with no keyframes between them. If the time falls between frame 5 and frame 6, the previous frame is 5 and the current frame is 6.

Let's start with the translation.

Translation

The first thing you do is find the current keyframe. This is done using a loop to increment the frame counter, starting at 0, while there are still translation keyframes, and while the time value for that current keyframe is less than your calculated elapsed time.

There are three possibilities for the value of the frame counter, as follows:

- The first is 0. This means that you need to simply copy the translation values for the very first translation keyframe into a temp variable holding the current translation.

- The second possibility for the frame counter is that it holds the number of the last keyframe. In this case, you do as you did for 0, except you use the last frame in the array of translation keyframes.

- The final and most likely value is the number of a keyframe in the middle of the two extremes. If this happens, you need to interpolate between this translation value of this keyframe and the translation value of the previous keyframe (framecounter - 1).

So just how do you do this? Remember linear interpolation from when you worked with formats such as md2? The same concept applies here.

All you need is the change in time between the two frames (∆t). Using this value, you can calculate the interpolation value to use when you perform linear interpolation. This is done using the following formula:

```
(CurrentTime - TimeOfPrevFrame)/∆t
```

You are subtracting the time of the previous frame from the current time and then dividing by the change in time between the two frames. Using the resultant value, you can easily interpolate between your X, Y, and Z translation values.

Rotation

Now for rotation. Rotation is almost the same process. The current and previous frames are calculated in the same way, and you follow nearly the same process if the model is at the extremes. If the model is at one of its extremes, meaning the current keyframe is equal to the very first or very last keyframe of the model, the rotation values of the last keyframe are placed into a temporary matrix using the SetRotation function of the CMatrix4X4 class.

The main difference shows up when you need to interpolate between rotations. Although you could use the same method as you did for translation, a much better and more graphically pleasing method involves using quaternions. If you skipped over Chapter 2, now would be a good time to read (or re-read) it.

Because the model stores its rotation angles as three Euler angles, the first thing to do is create two quaternions using the FromEulers function. You need to make two separate quaternions from the current and previous rotation keyframes. These two quaternions represent the rotations of each of the frames. Now, you must calculate the quaternion that represents the rotation at the current position. Once the interpolation value is calculated (it is done the same way as for translation), the quaternions can be fed into the SLERP function, along with the interpolation value, to create a new quaternion containing the correct rotation for the current time.

Because OpenGL uses matrices, it is necessary to convert the quaternion. A quaternion can then be turned back into a matrix using the ToMatrix4 function of the CQuaternion class.

After the rotation matrix is built, you need to add the translation to it. Using the same temp matrix you used for rotations, you can call the

SetTranslation function with the translation values you calculated earlier to finish it off.

There's only one step left before you can start drawing the model again. To find the joint's final matrix, you need to multiply the joint's local matrix (m_matLocal) by the temporary matrix you created. This result can be stored in m_matFinal, and is the matrix that will be used for transforming the vertices and normals later.

If you want, you can actually draw the bones alone now. The X, Y, and Z positions of the bones are stored in elements 12, 13, and 14 of the joint's final matrix. Drawing a line from this point to elements 12, 13, and 14 of the joint's parent's final matrix will give you an animated "skeleton" for the model, as Figure 6.3 shows.

Figure 6.3 *The animated skeleton of the model all by itself.*

Now that you have the new joint information, you must transform all the vertices and vertex normals. For clarity, all the code to transform and display the model is in the Cmas3d::RenderT() function. This function is called directly after the final matrices for all the joints are calculated.

As with the old render function, the meshes are drawn one at a time. For each mesh, the materials are first set up. Then, you move on to transforming the vertices and normals. You can start the rendering right away. As the faces are looped through, the ones that have no bones attached are drawn as normal, with no modifications whatsoever.

The rest of them, on the other hand, are different stories. A temporary vector is set up to hold both the new normal and the new vertex. First the normal must be taken care of. Because the matrix transformations actually modify the vector that is passed to them, the first thing to do is put the current normal into the temporary holder. After determining which joint the normal's vertex is attached to, you can use the `Transform3` function to modify the temporary normal, using only the rotation part of the matrix.

The vertex can be transformed in much the same way. The only major difference here is that the `Transform4` functions should be used, rather than `Transform3`. `Transform4` adds the translation in as well, giving the vertex its proper position.

Everything can now be sent to the rendering API. Don't forget to send the texture coordinates as well as the normal and vertex—make sure they are sent in the correct order!

Figure 6.4 shows the model in its full animating glory.

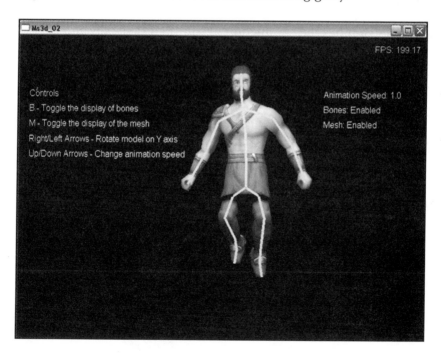

Figure 6.4 *The transformed model in mid-animation. Notice the bones that have been drawn over the top as a reference.*

As you notice in Figure 6.4, you can see the bones over the top of the model. In the demo this is done by disabling depth testing and drawing the bones using the technique put forward earlier. Just make sure you re-enable depth testing when you are done.

Well, there you have it. You can now load the *low polygon format,* which is my personal favorite. (A low polygon format simply means that it produces models with low polygon counts. Because you are dealing with games that must be rendered in real-time, low polygon models are a must. Using a high polygon model will slow down your game to the point of being unplayable.) I definitely suggest checking the editor and format out if you are an independent or money-strapped development team. It is quite nice, and comes at a great price.

Hope you enjoyed this chapter. Remember, if you have comments, questions, or suggestions, feel free to contact me at evan@codershq.com.

Conclusion

This chapter signifies the completion of your first skeletally animated format. You should now be able to load and use a very useful format that almost seems to be made just for games. You have learned how to animate bones by interpolating between their rotations and translation. You have also seen the most common use of quaternions in 3D game programming, interpolating between rotations.

Finally, the chapter tied it all together to create a fully working MS3D loader, complete with skeletal animation. Be sure to check out MilkShape's site at http://www.milkshape3d.com and check out the demo of MilkShape 3D on the CD (in the Software/MilkShape3d directory).

The next chapter covers one of the most popular formats, 3DS. You will learn how to load and render this fairly complicated format. You will learn how to use "chunk-based" formats. You will also catch a glimpse of some of the information that you can store in a file.

CHAPTER 7

THE 3DS MODELS

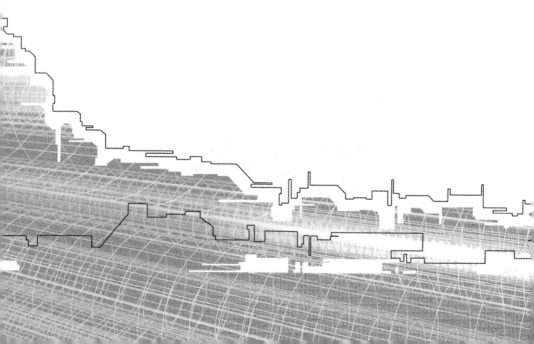

A s I browse various Internet forums, read mailing lists, and even just talk to various people about 3D models, this format seems to come up a lot. The questions "How do I load 3ds models?" and "How do I use 3ds models in my program?" show up all over the place.

Unfortunately, until now, there was not a very good reference on this format available. The references out there fell into one of three categories: libraries that offered you little control over what you could do, code and programs that are impossible to decipher, and confusing, very technical documents. Although this writing by no means covers everything to do with the 3ds format, my goal here is to get you started in the right direction.

This chapter guides you through loading and displaying a 3ds model exported directly from AutoDesk's 3ds format (http://www.autodesk.com). There is a ton of information contained in the 3ds files. This chapter extracts the data that will be most useful to you in your games or other 3D programs. This data includes the mesh data and material information, neglecting editor flags, lights, and other pieces. However, if you do feel you need these extras, it's a simple matter to add them after you get through this chapter.

Understanding Chunky 3ds Files

The format of a 3ds file is set up in a very interesting way. Each section of the file is its own "chunk". Each chunk contains an identifier, a length, and a group of bytes that holds the data for that chunk. Although other files had chunks, they either included a single header telling you where you would find each chunk or had the chunks set up in a specific order. A 3ds file does neither of these. The 3ds files can have the chunks in any order and there is no header telling you where they are located in the file or even how many of each chunk there is. The idea of this is shown in Figure 7.1, which illustrates a single file, made of up several chunks.

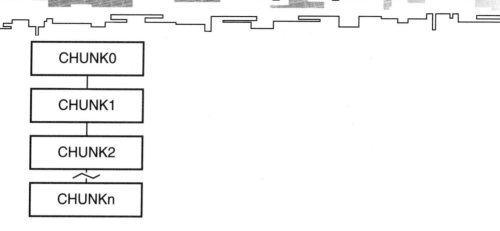

Figure 7.1   *A file made of chunks of data.*

This is fine and dandy until you look a little more in depth. The setup of a 3ds file can be very confusing at first glance. Not only is it split into many small chunks, but each chunk can have smaller sub-chunks, which may have even more sub-chunks. Worst of all, for the most part, the chunks need not be in any specific order in the file.

The structure of a 3ds file is set up more like Figure 7.2, rather than the format shown in Figure 7.1.

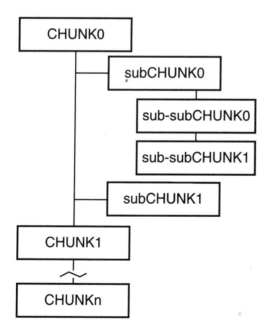

Figure 7.2   *A graphics representation of a file using a structure similar to 3ds.*

So just how do you handle that? The easiest way I have found is to first read in the header of the chunk. Each chunk in the 3ds file has a six-byte header that holds the identifier and length of the chunk. Then, based on the type of chunk and the length, a certain section of the program can be called to manipulate and process the data. A chunk can represent the meshes or triangles of an object, whereas sub-chunks of this chunk hold vertices, texture coordinates, and material information for that mesh. Other chunks can hold materials with sub-chunks for diffuse, specular, and ambient materials, with sub-chunks for each of the colors.

There are many benefits to handling it this way. First of all, it allows you to only process certain chunks. If a chunk contains data that is unneeded, you can simply read right past it. In the 3ds data files, for instance, you will probably want to skip over chunks that contain data that is relevant to the editor. Second, it makes it very easy to work with files such as 3ds models where the chunks are not in a set order. Because the header is read first, the type of chunk can be determined, and the appropriate actions can be taken by the code.

Last, this approach leads to a very modular program. If you need to change the specifications of a chunk or you add code for new chunks, it is a fairly simple process. It is very easy to find the section dealing with certain parts of the code. Adding code to deal with new types of chunks entails only tacking extra code onto the end.

This example program uses STL vectors quite a bit. If you need information on vectors, check out Appendix B, "STL Vector Primer," for a brief introduction or refresher.

3ds Chunk Headers: The Start

Each chunk in the 3ds file starts with a S3dsChunkHeader structure.

```
//------------------------------------------------
//- S3dsChunkHeader
//- Header for each chunk
struct S3dsChunkHeader
{
    unsigned short m_usID;
    unsigned int m_uiLength;
};
```

The first variable is the two-byte chunk identifier. This tells you what type of data the chunk contains. It can be vertex data, face data, animation data, even useless information data. The length variable is the length of the whole chunk, including the header. This can be a bit misleading however; the length value encompasses the current chunk plus the lengths of all the sub-chunks it contains, so be careful. Table 7.1 lists the most common chunk IDs along with their uses.

The 3ds Data File

The 3ds file is made up of many chunks, some of which are important for games, many which are not. In the following sections, you will learn about the most important chunks within a 3ds file. Using these chunks you can load, render, and texture a 3ds file. Although the first few chunks are guaranteed to be at the beginning of the file, the rest may pop up anywhere in the file, most of them any number of times.

Header 0x4D4D

Now you are ready to delve into the file itself. The first six bytes of the file should contain the main chunk's header. The ID of this header is 0x4d4d and the length variable should contain the total length of the file. This chunk contains all of the sub-chunks that make up the file. No action is necessary at this point; you can just move past the header and start reading chunks. Each 3ds model contains only one of these chunks.

The Version Chunk 0x0002

Somewhere in the file, generally the first sub-chunk (the 0x4D4D chunk), is this chunk. A total of 10 bytes in length, the data consists of a single four-byte integer containing the format version. It should be greater than 3. Older versions of 3ds Max differ from the newer versions in the way the file is set up, meaning that this program might not load them correctly.

Objects in the 0x4000 Chunk

The 0x4000 chunk contains data about objects. An object can be a triangle mesh, light, camera, or even window settings for the editor. For game programming, you generally want to neglect everything but the

Table 7.1　Common 3ds Chunks and Their Uses

ID Number	Use
0x4D4D	Used at the start of the file to signify that the file is a 3ds file.
0x0002	Holds the version number of the file.
0x4000	Contains an "object" such as a mesh, camera, or light. Each 0x4000 chunk contains sub-chunks with vertex, texture coordinate, and other information.
0x4100	A sub-chunk of 0x4000. A 0x4100 chunk contains everything needed to build a mesh of triangles.
0x4110	Contains the vertices for the object. It is a sub-chunk of 0x4100.
0x4120	Also a sub-chunk of 0x4100, a 0x4120 chunk contains the face information, including the vertex indexes that tell which vertices make up each face.
0x4130	Another sub-chunk of 0x4100, 0x4130 contains information on which materials are to be applied to which faces.
0x4140	Even another sub-chunk of 0x4100, this chunk contains the texture coordinates that allow a face to be texture mapped.
0xAFFF	A material definition is found inside 0xAFFF, colors for ambient, diffuse, and specular materials, as well as shininess and transparency are in this chunk.
0xA000	A sub-chunk of 0xAFFF that contains the material's name.
0xA010	A sub-chunk of 0xAFFF as well, contains the ambient color for the material.
0xA020	Another sub-chunk of 0xAFF, 0xA020 contains the diffuse color of the material.
0xA030	A fourth sub-chunk of 0xAFF, this contains the specular highlight colors for the specific material.
0xA040	Yet another 0xAFFF sub-chunk, this time contains the shininess of the material.
0xA050	Again, a sub-chunk of 0xAFFF that controls how transparent or opaque a material is.
0xA200	0xA200 is also a sub-chunk of the 0xAFFF chunk. This chunk stores the filename of the texture map or skin for the current material.

meshes. Loading lights and cameras could interfere with other parts of your game and lead to some very strange looking visual artifacts. However, you might want to look into loading and using the lights if you are interested in using the 3ds format for a level or world format.

The 0x4000 chunk contains a little bit of data by itself; the rest is wrapped up within sub-chunks. It contains a null-terminated string that stores the mesh name. Because the string's length is not set, it must be null terminated. Using strcpy on the data buffer can extract this name. However, if you are using a temporary pointer to move through the array, make sure you move it strlen(m_cName) + 1 bytes to account for the null terminator on the end of the string. After the string is read, the rest of the data length is full of sub-chunks. Keep in mind there may be a lot of meshes in the same file, so be sure to keep track of where you are.

```
//pseudocode to begin reading the 0x4000 chunk
if chunkID is 0x4000
read null terminated string (strcpy)
advance pointer past string and null pointer (strlen+1)
```

Triangular Mesh 0x4100

This is where the data you really want is. A triangular mesh chunk holds just that, a mesh containing triangles. A mesh is a group of polygons that make up a surface; a triangular mesh is the same except it consists of only triangles. In the 0x4100 chunk are the vertices, face, and texture coordinates, as well as the face material information.

Before you worry about reading in this data, you need a place to store it. That is where the S3dsMesh structure comes in. Each S3dsMesh structure holds one triangular mesh. Because the file does not reveal how many meshes there are total, you can call on the power of STL and std::vector to create a place to store any number of meshes.

Here is the mesh structure:

```
//------------------------------------------------
//- S3dsMesh
//- Group Mesh Data
struct S3dsMesh
{
    char m_cName[256];
```

```
    vector<S3dsVertex *> m_vVertices;
    vector<S3dsTexCoord *> m_vTexCoords;
    vector<S3dsFace *> m_vFaces;
    vector<S3dsObjMat *> m_vMaterials;
    unsigned short m_usNumFaces;
};
```

The first variable (m_cName) is the mesh name. This should be set when you first enter the 0x4000 chunk, because that is where the name string is located. You need to be careful here. The string within the 3ds model is unrestricted; it can be any length. However, in your structure there is only 256 bytes of storage. Hopefully, this will be enough to hold any of the mesh names, but be sure to check first. If the length of the string in the file exceeds 256 characters, you will need to truncate it before storing.

The rest of the data is contained in sub-chunks of the 0x4100 chunk. (Yes, you can have sub-chunks of sub-chunks!) Because you do not know how many vertices, faces, or materials there will be, you may want to use a std::vector. This is essentially a resizable array. Using std::vectors, you can add as many objects to your array as you like without allocating or resizing it. If you aren't sure about how to use std::vectors, I suggest you skip to Appendix B.

In the next section, you learn about the sub-chunks of the 0x4100 chunk. These chunks hold information about vertices, texture coordinates, faces, and materials. A particular object can have all of these sub-chunks, or just a few. An object doesn't have to contain texture coordinate and material information.

Vertices 0x4110

The 0x4110 sub-chunk of the 0x4100 chunk contains all of the vertex information for the mesh. This includes the X, Y, and Z coordinates for each vertex. (Thankfully, it does not contain another level of sub-chunks.) The vertices are stored in the mesh structure in the m_vVertices vector array.

Each vector is simply three floating-point values, wrapped in a structure for clarity. Here is the very simple, fairly boring S3dsVertex structure. You may notice that the vertex class here contains three floats, rather than a CVector3 class like the MS3D vertices did. I chose to do this for a reason. Because the vertices do not need to be transformed like those from

MS3D, there is no point in burdening your program with the extra files. In this case, a simple array of three floats will do well.

```
/ - - - - - - - - - - - - - - - - - - - - - - - - - - - - - - - - - - - - - - - - -
// - S3dsVertex
// - Vertex structure for 3ds models
struct S3dsVertex
{
    float m_fVert[3];
};
```

The first two bytes inside the 0x4110 chunk dictate the number of vertices in the mesh. Immediately following these two bytes are many sets of floating-point triples—an X, Y, and Z position for each vertex, which are read and stored as S3dsVertex structures.

Now, if you would like to check your progress, you can use the rendering function (C3ds::Render()) to render all the vertices as points. To do this, you must loop through the meshes one by one, and for each mesh, draw each vertex as a point in space.

Faces 0x4120

Another very important chunk is the 0x4120 chunk, or faces chunk. This chunk contains the vertex indexes for all the triangles in the current mesh; pretty important if you want a solid model. The faces are stored in the current mesh structure as well.

The S3dsFace structure is another fairly simple structure:

```
// - - - - - - - - - - - - - - - - - - - - - - - - - - - - - - - - - - - - - - - -
// - S3dsFace
// - Face of a 3ds model
struct S3dsFace
{
    unsigned short m_usIndices[3];   //Vertex indices
    CVector3 m_vecNormal;                //Face Normal
};
```

Now, you have to get these face components out of the file and into memory. As with the vertices, the first two bytes of the 0x4120 chunk are dedicated to holding the number of faces for the mesh (in this case, three). After that, there are the vertex indexes. There are three indexes for each triangle, one for each corner. That means there are three times the number of faces indexes. The m_vecNormal part of the face structure is not stored in the file; it must be calculated. This is done using the CalcFaceNormal function defined in model.h. This calculation will give you a unit vector perpendicular to the plane the triangle lies in. This value is required for lighting and materials when rendering.

The CalcFaceNormal function generates the face normal using the points of the triangle. First, two vectors are created from the points using an initial point of the first vertex and a final point as the second vertex for the first vector, and the third vertex for the second vector. The cross product of these vectors is then calculated. The resulting vector is perpendicular to the triangles, just like a normal vector. The only thing left to do is normalize the resulting vector so it can be sent to the rendering API.

These normals are only per face. To do smooth shading you will need per-vertex normals. A vertex normal can be calculated for a particular vertex by averaging the face normals of all of the faces that share that particular vertex.

You can now render the model as a solid object using just the vertex indexes. You can even send the normal vectors you calculated for each triangle and light the model as well.

Face Material Info 0x4130

Yet another level of sub-chunks. The face material information is a sub-chunk of the faces chunk (0x4120). One nice thing about the meshes in the 3ds files is that not only can you put different materials on different meshes like you could when using the MilkShape 3D format, but you can even put different materials on different parts of the same mesh. For example, a space ship made of a single mesh might need a different texture on the top of the ship than on the bottom. That's what the 0x4130 chunk is all about.

The S3dsObjMat stores information that defines which faces are to be covered with which materials. The 0x4130 chunk contains only indexes into the material array; it does not store the material information. Again, there is a vector of these structures in the mesh structure due to the fact that there could be more than one of them. The S3dsObjMesh structure contains an index into the materials array (which you will get to in a minute), as well as a list of face indexes that use this material.

```
//----------------------------------------------
//- S3ds Objmat
//- Structure that holds which faces go to a material
struct S3dsObjMat
{
    unsigned short m_usMatIdx;
    vector<unsigned short> m_vFaceIndices;
};
```

The data in the 0x4130 chunk is in the following order:

1. First, you see a null-terminated string that contains the name of the material to use. You can compare this string with the names of the materials loaded from the material chunks (0xAFFF, defined next). When the string matches, you can set the m_uiMatIdx variable to the index of that material. This will save a lot of time during rendering because you will not have to search for the proper material.

2. The now-familiar two-byte integer that tells you the number of faces that use this material is up next.

3. The number of two-byte integers, each representing a face, is last. Each number is an index into the faces array. A "0" corresponds with face 0, a "1" with face 1, and so on.

Now, when rendering the model, you must first set the material properties of the first material, render all the faces that use that material, switch to the next material, and repeat the rendering process until all the faces are drawn.

CAUTION

Do not use this chunk if you have not yet loaded the materials chunk. Doing so can cause unexpected behavior or crashes.

Texture Coordinates 0x4140 Chunk

The last important part of the mesh and the 0x4000 chunk is the 0x4140 sub-chunk. This sub-chunk holds the u and v texture mapping coordinates for each mesh vertex. These values position the texture on the triangle. They generally range from 0.0 to 1.0, but can go higher if the texture is to be repeated or tiled on the triangle. The first two bytes of the data give you the number of vertices. There are then two floating-point values for each vertex. These are stored in S3dsTexCoord structures, which are similar to the S3dsVertex structures, but contain only two floats rather than three.

There, all the geometry is now loaded. A relief isn't it? Wait, that is only half the battle. You still need to load all the material and texture information so you can make your models look much more interesting than a white, flat-shaded picture.

Materials 0xAFFF

To make your model more interesting and give it colors, highlights, and textures, you must load in the materials chunk. The materials chunk holds information about ambient, diffuse, and specular colors, as well as texture information and shininess. The mesh face chunks contain an index into this array of materials that specifies what materials are used for which model faces. The materials chunk is another conglomerate chunk, much like the 0x4000 mesh chunk. Even though it has lots of sub-chunks, I promise it's not as bad as the mesh chunk.

Let's take a look at the material structure right away:

```
//-------------------------------------------------
//- S3dsMaterial
//- Material structure
struct S3dsMaterial
{
    char m_cName[256];      //Name of material
    float m_fAmbient[4];   //Ambient color
    float m_fDiffuse[4];   //Diffuse color
    float m_fSpecular[4];  //Specular color
    float m_fShininess;    //Matl shininess
    CImage m_Texture;      //Texturemap
};
```

If you look in the C3ds class, there is a vector of S3dsMaterial structures, the same way there is a vector of meshes. This means there can be more than one material in the 3ds file, so again, as with the meshes, be sure to keep track of which material you are on.

The 0xAFFF material chunk does not contain any data of its own, only sub-chunks, which are defined in the following sections.

Material Name OxA000

The 0xA000 chunk contains the material's name. This is just a null-terminated string, same as the mesh name. It can be copied into the m_cName variable of the current material. Again, be careful that your material name does not exceed 256 characters. If it does, you must cut it off before you store it or you will overwrite the array and risk crashing your program.

Ambient Color OxA010

This chunk contains the ambient color of the current material. A sub-chunk 0x0011 contains the color in the form RGB, with one byte for each color value, for a total of three bytes. Before being stored in the m_fAmbient array, each element of the RGB color must be converted to a floating-point value between 0.0 and 1.0 so that they can be sent directly to the rendering API. This can be easily done using the formula (255 - R)/255, where R is the value for the red, green, or blue component of the color. The fourth value is always set to 1.0f in this case, because the value is not specified otherwise. The fourth value is included in the array so that it can be sent directly to the renderer, such as OpenGL. The following pseudo-code reads the ambient color, as well as the specular and diffuse colors.

```
//pseudocode to read colors for materials
read in three bytes of information, one for each red, green, and blue
convert each value to a floating point value between 0 and 1
store the new values in the first three appropriate array (m_fAmbient
for ambient color)
    set the fourth value of the array to 1.0 so that the whole array can
be sent to the rendering API
```

Diffuse OxA020 and Specular OxA030 Colors

The diffuse and specular colors work the same way as the ambient color, except they are stored in their own variables. Both have the same type of color chunks and values.

Shininess OxA040 and Transparency OxA050

A percentage sub-chunk gives these two values. The sub-chunk 0x0030 contains a single two-byte integer that ranges from 0 to 100 (the percentage). Dividing by 100 returns the floating-point value to between 0 and 1. The shininess percentage (0 percent being dull, 100 percent being as shiny as possible) goes into the m_fShininess variable; the transparency is the fourth value in the m_fDiffuse array.

```
//pseudo code to read shininess and transparency
Read shininess chunk
Convert shininess to a value between 0 and 1 by dividing by 100
Set shininess parameter equal this value
Read the transparency value
Convert shininess into a value from 0 to 1 in the same way as transparency
Set the fourth value in the diffuse color array equal to the resulting value
```

Texture Map 0xA200 and 0xA300

The last and probably the most important chunk of the material is the texture. The texture is the "skin" that covers the model and contains details too difficult to create only with triangles and colors. This gives the model a definite look, enhancing believability and realism.

The texture map structure starts with a chunk of type 0xA200. This 0xA200 or texture map chunk contains sub-chunks as well, although the only sub-chunk one you need is 0xA300. It contains a null-terminated string that specifies the texture's filename. This string can be fed directly into the Load function of the CImage class contained within the material structure. If you are not using the CImage class included in the basecode, you can extract this string with strcpy and store it in a temporary buffer to pass to your own image-loading functions.

```
//Reading and loading the texture filename
Set a pointer (char *) equal to the start of the data in the 0xA300
chunk.
Pass this pointer to the CImage::Load() function.
```

Whew, you now have *all* the static data you need to at least render the model with light and texture.

Rendering Your 3ds Files

Let's take a look at how to pull all the data you have loaded together and put it onto the screen. You must deal with many issues while rendering. Some meshes have material information stored in them; some meshes have no materials at all. Some meshes might not contain any triangles, due to the fact they are made for cameras and lights. You must consider and deal with all of these circumstances.

The best way to visualize how these files are rendered is to look at a flow chart. The rendering flow is shown in Figure 7.3. Take a look at it before you read on.

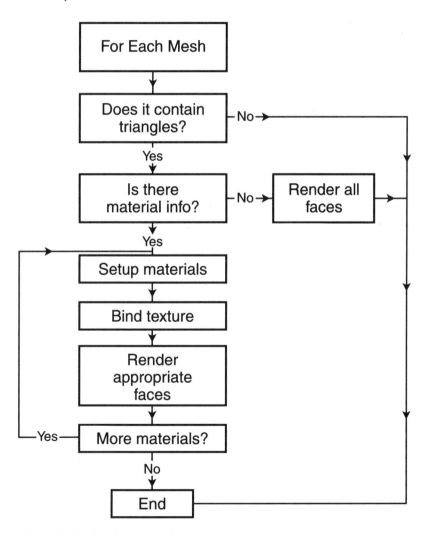

Figure 7.3 *Rendering flowchart.*

Your rendering function must contain a loop that loops through each of the meshes and draws them if necessary.

The first thing you must determine is whether the current mesh contains any face information. This can be done by checking the size of the face array. If it is 0, just skip the mesh altogether and continue. If it contains no triangles, it is not a valid triangle-mesh.

You must next determine how different parts of the model are rendered. If there is information in the m_vObjMat variable, the mesh contains material information and it must be set up first. If this branch is taken, a new loop must be set up to loop through all of the ObjMat objects so the proper material is applied to the proper faces.

Then, using the material index, you must set up the material properties. Make sure to enable blending, lighting, and to bind the texture as well. If you are using OpenGL, the materials are specified using the glMaterialf function, and blending is enabled using the glEnable function with the parameter GL_BLEND. Make sure to set your blending function using this code:

```
glBlendFunc(GL_SRC_ALPHA, GL_ONE_MINUS_SRC_ALPHA);
```

As for the texture, you can use the CImage::Bind() function if you are using the CImage class, or glBindTexture if you are using another image-loading routine.

Then, you can render the faces specified by the current material information.

If there are no materials for the specified object, you can now render the faces. Because leaving blending enabled can cause undefined results, it is best to disable it when you take this route. You should also disable texturing as well.

In the C3ds::Render function, I use immediate mode to send vertex, texture coordinates, and normal information to OpenGL. There are better ways to do this; for instance using vertex arrays. I decided to leave it this way to make it easier to understand, particularly if you do not know OpenGL well.

Conclusion

This chapter should contain plenty of information to get you going. You can now load and render a 3ds model, complete with textures and materials. You also have been introduced to a format that uses a system of independent chunks to create the file. Now you should be able to look at the full 3ds format, which can be obtained from a site such as http://www.wotsit.org, and be able to load and utilize any of the extra chunks stored in the file that were not covered here. The 3ds format stores a ton of information and holds endless possibilities. The next chapter shows you how to create a loader for Half-Life's MDL format using basecode released by VALVe software. That chapter uses existing basecode rather than creating an entire loader from scratch due to the complexity of the format. Read on to find out how to load this popular, powerful format.

CHAPTER 8

MDL, THE LEGENDARY HALF-LIFE FORMAT

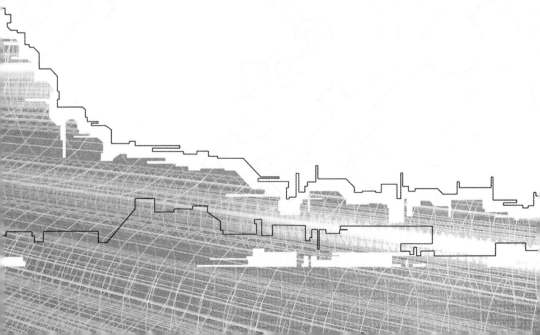

J ust about everyone has played, or at least seen, *Half-Life*. This groundbreaking game from VALVe software became an instant success, eventually spawning the insanely popular counter-terrorism mod *Counter-Strike* (www.counter-strike.net). Figure 8.1 shows *Half-Life* in action.

Figure 8.1 *VALVe software's legendary Half-Life in action. Half-Life rocked the gaming world with its then groundbreaking graphics, AI, and of course its realistic skeletal animations. Here, a scary alien slave readies a deadly blast of electricity.*

Not only did Half-Life offer a refreshing change of pace from the rush-around-with-guns-blazing 3D games of the time, it was quite revolutionary for its time. Not only was it one of the first mainstream games to incorporate skeletal animation, it had an intriguing story, scripted sequences, and great graphics to boot. Best of all, it even ran on my old 133MHz computer.

In my opinion, I think this is another great format to use due to the popularity of the game. Because of this, there are a great number of free models available at places such as PolyCount (http://www.polycount.com) and FilePlanet (www.fileplanet.com), as well as a large number of people creating new data for various modifications.

This chapter takes a slightly different approach. Instead of writing a full loader from scratch, you will be using code files prepared by VALVe software. These files are part of the Half-Life SDK. The reason for this is that the Half-Life format is very, very complex.

VALVe's MDL Viewer Files

Using the files from VALVe's MDL viewer requires a little tweaking before they will work with your basecode. The first thing to do is go into mdlviewer.cpp and gut out all of the functions. These are the initialization and main loop functions for a standalone viewer. Because you are going to be using your own main loop and your own basecode, their main loop and basecode has to go. The main() function and all of its associated parts must be removed to make way for your own.

Also, any references to the glut library (glut.h and glut**) need to be removed. This was also left in for the standalone viewer. All functions that begin with "glut", such as glutMainLoop() and glutInputfunc, need to be removed. After these functions are gone, you can remove glut.h as well.

This has already been done for you in the included files, found on the CD in the Code/Chapter 8/hl_src directory. To use the MDL loading code, you need the following files (all included on the CD with the demo in the hl_src folder of the demo):

```
Code/Chapter 8/hl_src /math.cpp
Code/Chapter 8/hl_src /mathlib.h
Code/Chapter 8/hl_src /mdlviewer.cpp
Code/Chapter 8/hl_src /mdlviewer.h
Code/Chapter 8/hl_src /studio.h
Code/Chapter 8/hl_src /studio_renderer.cpp
Code/Chapter 8/hl_src /studio_utils.cpp
```

Once all these files are included into your project (copy the hl_src directory into your project directory), you are ready to start working.

Initializing the Model

First things first, let's load the model and get it set up. First of all you need an instance of the StudioModel class to work with. StudioModel is the name of the class containing everything to do with the models, just as CMd2, Cms3d, and others were in previous chapters.

Loading the model is simple. Using the Init function of your StudioModel instance, you pass it a filename. The class takes care of loading everything from there. It doesn't get much simpler than that! Here is the actual code to initialize the model file "pirate.mdl":

```
g_MDL.Init("pirate.mdl");
```

Before you can jump right to rendering, there are several more pieces you must initiate. First is the animation sequence. An animation sequence in the Half-Life MDL files contains one "action". This may be running, jumping, crouching, or any other action.

Using the SetSequence function, you can set the current animation sequence. Because it's the beginning of the program, I set it to 0 in my code:

```
//Set the current animation sequence to 0
g_MDL.SetSequence(0);
```

Next you need to initialize the programmable bone controllers. These controllers provide a bit of extra functionality to the model. Using the SetController function, I set all four of the controllers to 0.0. I recommend that you play with the values just to see what they do; maybe a great idea will come to your mind.

```
//Set all bone controllers to 0
g_MDL.SetController(0, 0.0);
g_MDL.SetController(1, 0.0);
g_MDL.SetController(2, 0.0);
g_MDL.SetController(3, 0.0);
```

Last, the mouth position is set. The SetMouth function, as you might imagine, effects the position of the model's mouth. By modifying this value during the game you can create a model that appears to be speaking. Done carefully, it is even possible to get the lips synced with the actor's voice:

```
//Set the mouth position to 0
g_MDL.SetMouth(0);
```

Rendering the MDL Code

Now the minute you have all been waiting for! Rendering. Displaying the MDLs onscreen is nearly as easy as loading them. A simple call to DrawModel puts the model onto the screen. Just calling DrawModel, however, will not produce any animation. Here's the code:

```
// Draw the model without any animation
g_MDL.DrawModel();
```

Animating the Model

To actually animate the model, you need a timer. The AdvanceFrames function of the StudioModel class takes the change in time from the last frame to the current one. Using the CTimer class from the basecode makes this really easy to find. Calling the GetSeconds function returns the number of seconds that have elapsed since it was last called. By calling this function and feeding the results into the AdvanceFrame function, you animate the model. You can even vary the speed of the animation by multiplying the elapsed time by a speed value. A speed value of 1.0 gives you the original speed, 2.0 gives you twice the speed, and so on. Be sure to call the DrawModel function sometime after the AdvanceFrame call or you will get a black screen. Here is the code that uses a CTimer function to retrieve the number of seconds since the last frame—it then uses that value in the Animate function:

```
//Get the number of seconds that have elapsed since the last frame
//Multiplying this value by a speed multiplier will slow
// down or speed up the animation of the model.
float fSec = g_Timer.GetSeconds() * fTimeMult;
//Advance the model's animation using the value you just calculated
g_MDL.AdvanceFrame(fSec);
//Draw the model at its new position
g_MDL.DrawModel();
```

That was pretty easy wasn't it? Just for kicks, Figure 8.2 shows the MDL loader in action.

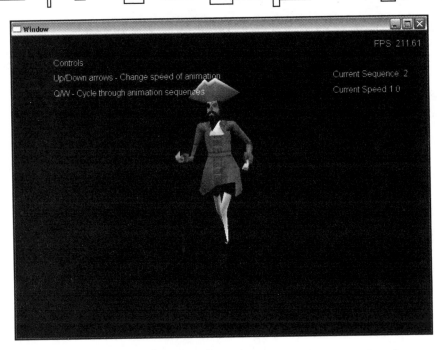

Figure 8.2   *The MDL loader in action. The Half-Life format is a very complicated and powerful format.*

For More Practice...

If you feel up to looking at VALVe's code and deciphering parts of the format yourself, try these projects:

- Extract and replace the internal textures.
- Extract the skeleton and replace it with one for a file (decompile it).
- Create your own format out of it by dropping out everything you don't need.
- Figure out how to use the attachments (hint, look at md3 first).

Overall, MDL is an interesting, but very complicated, format. It contains data to do almost everything under the sun. From blending animations, to weapons attachment, to embedded textures, MDL has it all.

Enter the MDL format at your own risk :)

Conclusion

Although this is a short introduction to such a powerful format, it's a good start to help you use it within your own games and programs. VALVe created an extremely powerful, but also an extremely complex, file format. The bone and mouth controllers can provide very specific control over the model. Using the mouth controller, you can set up a rudimentary lip-syncing system without creating a new format or changing the core code that actually loads the model.

The next chapter covers id Software's MD3 format. The MD3 format is another very popular format due to its use in id Software's own *Quake III* as well as many games that use the *Quake III* engine licensed from id. MD3 is another good format to use in your games. Read on!

CHAPTER 9

ENTER THE QUAKE! QUAKE III's MD3 FORMAT

Back at the beginning of the book you learned about the MD2 format used in id Software's *Quake II*. Since then, *Quake* and its file format have matured. MD2's bigger brother, MD3, was created for use in *Quake III*.

Quake III pushed games ahead with more and prettier graphics features, such as curved surfaces. The new MD3 format has the capability to "connect" with other models through the use of tags. The characters in Quake III make use of this system with a different model for the head, torso, and legs. This allows different parts of the body to be running different animation sequences, and can also allow for mix-and-match players if implemented correctly. Figure 9.1 shows id Software's Quake III in action.

Figure 9.1   *id Software's Quake III* (http://www.idsoftware.com), just one of the many games built around the Quake III engine.

This is another good format to use because nearly all games based off the Quake III engine (such as American McGee's *Alice* and *Return to Castle Wolfenstein*) use the MD3 format as well. This makes for many resources, due to the strong mod community. Members of the gaming community create many new and extra models. Because so many games use this format, many new models are also created in this format.

Retrieving Data

As with all of the model formats, before you can render or animate anything, you must have the data out of the file. MD3 contains many data structures that are similar to MD2's, but beware, there are differences. It is best not to try to modify your MD2 code to load MD3s, but rather start from scratch.

The MD3 format is set up with a very specific structure. Starting with the header and going all the way through the mesh data, it is set up much like the MD2 files. Figure 9.2 shows the organization of the MD3 file.

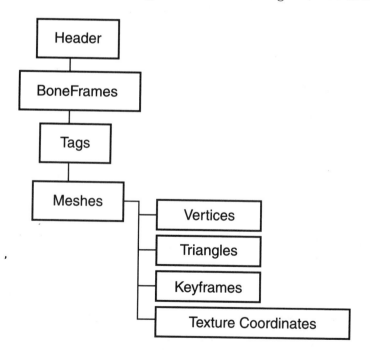

Figure 9.2 *The general structure of the MD3 file. This shows what an MD3 file holds, in what order it holds information, and the general layout of the file.*

The MD3 Header

The MD3 header is very similar to MD2's header. It contains an ID, a version number, and information about various chunks in the file. Check out the definition of the header:

```
//----------------------------------------------------------
//- SMd3Header
//- File header for the md3 file, similar to md2
struct SMd3Header
{
    int m_iId;              //Must be IDP3 (860898377)
    int m_iVersion;         //Must be 15
    char m_cFilename[68];   //Full filename
    int m_iNumFrames;       //Number of animation keyframes
    int m_iNumTags;         //Number of tags
    int m_iNumMeshes;       //Number of sub-meshes
    int m_iMaxSkins;        //Maximum number of skins for model
    int m_iHeaderSize;      //Size of this header
    int m_iTagOffset;        //File offset for tags
    int m_iMeshOffset;         //End of tags
    int m_iFileSize;        //Size of file
};
```

Quite a bit of stuff. Check out Table 9.1 for an explanation about how each variable within the header is used.

Then come two more integers that dictate the start and end positions of the tag structures. Again, you'll get to tags later on in the chapter.

The very last variable is another integer that holds the total file size of the model.

Boneframes

The next part of the file (directly after the header) contains what are called *boneframes*. Each boneframe is a total of 56 bytes and holds information concerning bounding boxes for the model. There is one boneframe for each keyframe of animation, meaning that the boneframes contain the bounding information for each frame. The first twelve bytes are the minimum X, Y, and Z values of the bounding box, whereas the second twelve bytes are the maximum values.

Table 9.1 MD3 Header Values

Variable	Purpose
m_iID	This variable identifies the file as an MD3 model. The value of this variable is "IDP3", which translates to 860898377.
m_iVersion	Should always be equal to 15. If either the first or second variables are not what they are supposed to be, the model is not valid.
m_cFilename	This array of characters holds the filename of the model relative to the BASEQ3 directory of Quake III. This is generally of little use if you are using the model for your own applications.
m_iNumFrames	This variable holds the number of keyframes that are used in the model for purposes of animation.
m_iNumTags	Here you will find the number of tags, or attachment points, stored in the MD3 model. Tags allow you to attach one MD3 model to another.
m_iNumMeshes	Each MD3 contains at least one mesh, or geometry data, chunk. However, this variable will let you know if the model contains just the required one, or two or more submeshes.
m_iMaxSkins	This variable tells you the maximum number of skins this MD3 model can use.
m_iHeaderSize	The total length of this file header can be found by reading this variable. This value will also tell you the offset, in bytes, from the start of the file to the boneframes.
m_iTagOffset	To read the tags, you must know where in the file they are located. This variable will give you a value, in bytes, that will allow you to seek out the tag structures buried in the model file.
m_iMeshOffset	Like the tag offset tells you where to find the tags, the mesh offset tells you where to find the mesh data within the MD3.
int m_iFilesize	The last variable in the header. It contains the total size, in bytes, of the MD3 file. This is useful for verifying that all of the data is here and to help determine whether the file has been tampered with.

Each of the X, Y, and Z values is a four-byte floating-point number. Using these six values you can construct a full bounding box for the model. Next comes the X, Y, Z coordinates of the origin. This set of three floats gives you the center of the bounding box. Although it is typically 0, 0, 0, it can vary. The minimum and maximum values of the box are relative to this point.

Next comes a floating-point value, which holds the radius of the bounding sphere for the model. Like the bounding box, the center of this sphere is determined by the origin specified. A bounding sphere provides a faster way to quickly check whether a model might be colliding with an object such as the world or another model.

Last there are 16 bytes that make up the boneframe's name. This name has no real purpose in the game, but can be helpful for the artists who are creating the model.

MD3 Tag Structures

Next in line are the tag structures, used to connect models together. The tag structures in MD3 are used when attaching two models together, such as when attaching a character's legs to its torso or a weapon to a character. Each tag consists of a 3×3 rotation matrix, a position vector, and a 64-character name. The name is simply a string that identifies the tag. Common names for tags include Weapon01, Torso, and Head; each designates what kind of model is meant to be attached to the specific tag. The rotation matrix stores the rotation value for the specific frame. This matrix will tell the attached models how much to rotate. For instance, the attached weapon must rotate if the wrist it is attached to is rotated. Although the rotations are stored in the file as a 3×3 matrix, it is helpful to convert the matrix to a quaternion when you read it in.

Converting the matrix to a rotation quaternion will allow you to take advantage of the quaternion interpolations when animating the model. The last value, the position vector, gives the current position of the tag. It is used to keep the models attached together. The position vector changes when one part of the model changes positions, requiring the other parts to keep up. This happens, for example, when the character crouches, at which point the torso must also move downward to stay on top of the legs.

As mentioned previously, a much better way to efficiently store these tags, as well as cut down on processing time, is to store the rotation matrix as a quaternion. Using the `FromMatrix` function of the quaternion class, the rotation matrix can be converted into a quaternion after being read from the file. After converting the data from the file into a matrix, you can call the `FromMatrix` function included with the `CQuaternion` class. By passing your rotation matrix to this function, it will fill in the quaternion data for you.

Here is what you finally end up with for a data structure:

```
//------------------------------------------------------
//- SMd3Tag
//- Tag structure for Md3
struct SMd3Tag
{
    char m_cName[64];    //Name of tag
    CVector3 m_vecPos;   //Position of the tag
    //Even though the file contains a 3x3 matrix
    //It is converted into a quaternion before being stored in memory
    // to conserve space and take advantage of quaternion interpolation
    CQuaternion m_qRot;  //Rotation for the frame
};
```

The number of tags in each set is determined by the `m_iNumTags` variable in the file's header. Because the tags are used for animation, there is one set of tags for every frame of animation. If there are 100 frames of animation, and there is one tag to attach the weapon to, one to attach the head, and one to attach the legs, there will be a total of 300 tags. (Three for each of the 100 keyframes.) To get the total number of tags, you only need to multiply the `m_iNumTags` and the `m_iNumFrames` variables that are stored in the header of the MD3 file.

Meshes

Meshes contain the real meat of the file (or any model file format for that matter). The meshes contain everything seen on the screen. The MD3 meshes contain all the vertex, animation, face, and texture information, a lot like MD2 does. The difference here between MD2 and MD3 is that MD3 can have multiple meshes. The number of meshes in each file is given by the `m_iNumMeshes` variable in the file header. Multiple meshes can be useful if you want to apply different types of animations to different parts of the model. The arms may be a separate mesh from the torso because it might be easier for the artist to animate each part separately. Another instance in which multiple meshes can be used is when parts of the model are not connected to other parts of the model and must move independently.

Each mesh is independent of the rest and is set up in a specific order, as shown in Figure 9.3. Because each mesh is independent, you can treat it as its own 3D model. Each mesh contains its own animation data, and its own vertices, texture coordinates, and triangles. A mesh will never need to access data from other meshes, even within the same file.

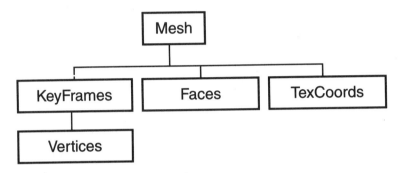

Figure 9.3   *The MD3 mesh layout. Each mesh chunk consists of faces and texture coordinates as well as keyframes. Each keyframe contains a set of vertices for that position.*

Take a look at the following mesh structure:

```
//---------------------------------------------------------
//- SMd3Mesh
//- A single mesh in the md3 file
struct SMd3Mesh
{
    SMd3MeshHeader m_Header;
    SMd3KeyFrame * m_pKeyFrames;
    SMd3Face * m_pFaces;
    SMd3TexCoord * m_pTexCoords;
    SMd3Skin * m_pSkins;
};
```

Quite a bit of stuff here! A header, animation data, faces, texture coordinates, and more. There is a pointer for each of the sections, other than the header, which means that you must allocate memory for each section. Each section, including the header, keyframes, faces, texture coordinates, and skins, are explained in their own sections that follow.

For the sake of simplicity, I chose not to use std::vectors here. Because of this, if you look at the code, you will see a constructor and destructor so the structure will clean up after itself when the program exits.

The Mesh Header

The mesh header tells you everything you need to do to find and load all of the data. The header structure is 108 bytes long and contains the number of each component, and offset into the mesh data for each component as well. Here is the structure code; Table 9.2 contains the mesh header values:

```
//-------------------------------------------------
//- SMd3MeshHeader
//- Header for each mesh in the md3 file
struct SMd3MeshHeader
{
    char m_cMeshId[4];      //Mesh ID
    char m_cName[68];       //Mesh name
    int m_iNumMeshFrames;   //Number of animation frames in mesh
    int m_iNumSkins;        //Number of skins for this mesh
    int m_iNumVerts;        //Number of vertices
    int m_iNumTriangles;    //Number of triangles
    int m_iTriOffset;       //Offset for the triangles
    int m_iHeaderSize;      //Size of this header
    int m_iUVOffset;        //Texture coordinate offset
    int m_iVertexOffset;    //Offset for the vertices
    int m_iMeshSize;        //Total size of the mesh
};
```

Most of this is straightforward, but there are a few things you need to be careful of. The first is to be sure you are reading from the correct place in the file. The offsets in this header are offsets in bytes from the beginning of the mesh chunk itself, not the start of the file or the last piece of data read. The second is to be sure that you store the data in the

> **CAUTION**
>
> Just to reiterate: the offsets in this header are offsets in bytes from the beginning of the *mesh chunk* itself, not the start of the file or the last piece of data read. Be sure to remember this so that you read from the correct place in the file.

Table 9.2 Mesh Header Values

Variable	Purpose
m_cMeshId[4]	A four-byte ID for the mesh; can be ignored.
m_cName[68]	A 68-character mesh name; can also be ignored.
m_iNumMeshFrames	This four-byte integer stores the number of keyframes contained within the mesh.
m_iNumSkins	Another four byte integer. This time, it stores the number of skins that are used to texture this particular mesh.
m_iNumVerts	Yet another four-byte integer. This variable gives you the number of vertices that each keyframe will contain.
m_iNumTriangles	A four-byte integer again. It stores the number of triangles that make up the mesh.
m_iTriOffset	Tells you how far into the mesh the triangle information can be found.
m_iHeaderSize	Holds the total size of this header.
m_iUVOffset	Tells the program where to find the U/V texture coordinates within the mesh.
m_iVertexOffset	Tells the offset into the mesh where the first of the vertices and keyframes can be found. Because this value will take you to the start of the keyframes, you can also think of it as the keyframe offset.
m_iMeshSize	Holds the total size of the mesh in bytes, header and all.

correct format and in the correct place. Nothing is worse than corrupting or losing data.

Before you can go on, you need to know the format of all the data in the mesh structure, or it will not do you any good. Let's start with the skins.

Skins

This is the simplest structure within the MD3 file. It contains only a 68-character string that holds the path and name of the texture file. Because the texture filename is relative to the `baseq3` path, which you probably won't have, I would advise you to hack off the pathname, and keep only the filename. It will make your life a lot easier. Another problem you may encounter is filenames without extensions. With Quake III, this means the model uses a shader for the particular mesh instead of a regular texture. A Quake III shader is a text file, generally with a .shader extension on it. These files contain texture information such as animations and special effects.

If you come across one of these cases, you will need to do one of two things. You will need to create a texture to take the place of the shader or you will need to write a routine to read and parse the shader information to determine, at the very least, the texture filenames. The shader file can contain many other pieces of data, including multitexturing information, deformations, and texture effects. Although they do not have to be loaded, they can add a lot of detail and realism to a model.

> **NOTE**
>
> Shaders are beyond the scope of this book, and there are many good resources on the Web about them. One of the best is the *Shader Bible*, created by Paul Jaquays and Brian Hook. It's available online at `http://qeradiant.com/manual/Q3AShader_Manual/`.

KeyFrames and Vertices

These two sections, keyframes and vertices, go hand in hand in an MD3 file. An MD3 keyframe is nothing but a collection of vertices that define where the model is and what it looks like at a particular time.

A model may have a set of keyframes that, when cycled through, make the model appear to be walking or jumping, or doing some other action. Each keyframe stores its own set of vertex positions rather than just storing ones that are moved or updated from frame to frame. This approach is a lot like taking snapshots of the model's vertices at certain intervals and using these snapshots to animate the model later.

Let's get right to the structures:

```
//----------------------------------------------------------
//- SMd3Vertex
//- A single vertex in the MD3 file
struct SMd3Vertex
{
    float m_fVert[3];
};
//----------------------------------------------------------
//- SMd3KeyFrame
//- A single animation keyframe, contains new vertex positions
struct SMd3KeyFrame
{
    SMd3Vertex * m_pVertices;
};
```

This is where you need to be careful. Even though you want the vertices as floats, the MD3 files do not store them this way.

Each vertex takes up eight bytes, instead of twelve, to save space. The X, Y, and Z components are two bytes each. To move from this format to your three-float format, you divide each component of the vertex by 64.0f—FinalX = OriginalX / 64.0f—and store it in the appropriate place.

The number of keyframes in a mesh is stored in the mesh's header, as the m_iNumMesh frames variable, and the number of vertices in each frame is contained in the m_iNumVerts variable. Don't forget to use the offset given to you in the header before you start reading in data.

Faces

As with the vertices and keyframes, be sure to jump to the triangle offset as given in the header before you start getting data, lest you have disastrous results. As with MD2, all faces in the MD3 model are triangles. Each face structure contains three unsigned shorts that hold indexes into the arrays of vertices.

There is only one set of faces per mesh; the same indexes are used regardless of which keyframe of animation is being rendered.

Texture Coordinates

Models are pretty boring without textures on them. To use textures, you need texture coordinates. The texture coordinates for each mesh are stored at the offset given by the mesh header. Each texture coordinate is simply two floating-point values, one for each u and v. These coordinates will allow you to have more realistic models, without using too many polygons. The texture can add details that the polygons cannot.

Once you have all this data, you can render and animate the model.

Basic Rendering and Animating

I am not going to go over this in great detail because everything in the MD3 file can be rendered in the same way as an MD2 file. As you loop through each mesh, the faces can be drawn in a traditional manner. Using the vertex indexes stored in the face structures, as well as the texture coordinates, it is very easy to get the model onto the screen. Check out the CMd3::Render function for the exact code. Using the CMd3::Render function is very simple; here's an example of it:

```
//Rendering an MD3 model
//The Render function only renders one frame of the model
g_Md3Model.Render(frameNum);
```

Animating the model is also similar to MD2. Using a timer, you calculate an interpolation value and use it to linearly interpolate between the two nearest keyframes. This must be done for each mesh. The simplest way to render the new, interpolated vertices is just to send each to the renderer as soon as it is generated. This method avoids storing the interpolated vertices, even temporarily. The vertices can be sent one by one using a function such as glVertex3f in OpenGL.

If you want to use vertex arrays or other optimization techniques, you might need to store the vertices in a temporary buffer before sending them off to the rendering API. For a little more information and applicable code, check out the CMd3::Animate function in the first demo. The first demo found in the /Code/Chapter9 directory shows the basic rendering and animation discussed here. Figure 9.4 shows a single MD3 model being animated by itself.

Figure 9.4   *A single-part MD3 model in mid-animation.*

Using Multi-Part Models

The biggest advantage of the MD3 format is its ability to use multi-part models. A multi-part model combines two or more models into one. This is beneficial when you need to mix and match models such as using two torsos and two sets of legs to create four unique models, rather than just two. It also allows you to link weapons or other attachments to a character or object without having to create custom animations for either the original model or the one being attached. Using those mysterious tag structures you loaded in earlier, you can attach one model to another at predefined points.

You can have one model for the legs of the character and another for the torso. When connected together using the tags, they would look and act like a single model. However, each part of the model can be animated individually. The legs can be playing a running animation while the torso is playing a shooting animation, thus allowing the character to run and shoot at the same time. This feature alone has many advantages. In the case of a first-person shooter using a traditional model format such as MD2, the artist would need to make a jump-and-shoot animation, a run-and-shoot animation, a walk-and-shoot animation, and so on.

With MD3 however, a single shooting animation with the torso can be played along with a running, walking, or jumping animation on the attached legs. This also allows artists to make three leg models and four torso models that can be mixed and matched by the programmers to create a variety of characters.

The second demo (found in /Code/Chapter9/) contains all the code for using multi-part models. Keep in mind that using this code does not prevent you from using single-part models. The code from this demo works just as well with both.

Tags

As I mentioned earlier, you finally get to use those tags you loaded from the file. These tags will help you assemble the model together by providing information about how to transform each of the models so that they all stay properly attached. Without tags, attaching legs to a torso can be very difficult because when the torso moves upward, the legs may not, creating a significant visual artifact. A good way to think about the tags is as joints in a skeletal animation system. These tags contain parent nodes and child nodes, just as with regular skeletal animation.

Interpolation

The first thing you need to do is modify the CMd3::Animate function. Just like the mesh keyframes, the tag positions and rotations must be interpolated as well. Because there is one tag for every frame, the last and next frame indexes, the interpolation values calculated for interpolating between the mesh keyframes can be reused here. This time, rather than sending each vertex to the rendering API as it is calculated, it may help to store them temporarily. This allows you to better control the vertices and allows you to implement features such as vertex arrays in the optimization process.

The CMd3::Animate function only needs to be modified slightly. Because you are using the tags now, they must be interpolated along with the rest of the model. This can be accomplished in the same way as regular skeletal animation—using linear interpolation for the positions and a quaternion SLERP function for the rotations.

Each tag "frame" consists of two important parts:

- The *position* is stored in a three-element vector. For the purpose of interpolation, the position can be treated as a single vertex of the mesh.

- The *rotation* is stored in the form of a unit quaternion. The rotation quaternion should be SLERPed in order to give the rotation interpolation a smooth curve. This is done using the SLERP function provided in the math code used throughout the book. Just plug in the quaternion from the previous frame, the quaternion from the next frame, and the interpolation value, and the SLERP function will spit out a new quaternion.

Attaching One Model to Another

Next, you need some way to attach one model to another. This is done using the CMd3::Attach function. The Attach function specifies a pointer to another CMD3 model, and an integer denoting which tag it should be attached to. The Attach function takes this pointer and stores it in an array of pointers known as the child-model array. The child-model array contains one pointer for each tag on the model. All of the pointers in the array start out as NULL, but when a model is attached to that particular joint, the pointer is changed to point to the attached model instead. An example of attaching one model to another using the CMd3::Attach() model is shown here:

```
//Attach a model called g_Weapon to g_Character at the
//first tag
g_Character.Attach(g_Weapon, 0);
```

Models are always attached to their parents, not the other way around. Generally, the root joints of a humanoid character are the legs. The torso model is attached to the legs, the head and weapons models are attached to the torso, and so forth.

Drawing the Multi-Part Model

Now that you have one model attached to another, it is time to draw them. The first thing to do is to remove any drawing code from the Animate function. Now you can call the animate functions in each frame, but it will simply calculate the interpolated vertices and tags and store them.

The RenderT() function is where all the action takes place. When the RenderT() function of a parent joint is called, the parent joint's meshes are rendered as normal. Then, for each tag that contains a pointer to a child mesh, a 4x4 transformation matrix is built using the interpolated quaternion and position values of the tag. The rendering API can then be set up to render the mesh in the correct position and with the correct orientation.

This can be accomplished by pushing a new matrix onto the stack, using a call such as glPushMatrix in OpenGL. Using the new copy of the view matrix you just created, multiply it by the transformation matrix you created from the tag data. This will give you the proper position and orientation to render the first child mesh. A child mesh could be used for a weapon attached to the character's hand, or even perhaps to allow the character's head to move in sync with its torso.

Because the RenderT() function is recursive, if the child mesh you render has a child of its own, the same thing will happen again. This process will continue down the line until a mesh is reached that has no children. The function then backs up, popping the matrices off the stack as it goes, back to the original parent node. Then, it continues the loop if there are more lines of child models to render. In this way, every child down the line gets the combined transformation of every parent before it.

Figure 9.5 shows a picture of a multi-part character model being rendered. The legs, torso, and head are all separate MD3 models with separate animations. If a weapon were present, it would also be its own MD3 model with separate animations.

Conclusion

After finishing this chapter, you should be able to create an MD3 loader for your engine or game. With loading and animation capabilities, you are ready to tell your artists to start churning out MD3s for your new game. You can even use the attachment points to build full characters and to attach weapons or other models to your characters.

The next chapter takes you through some tips and tricks that can be used with your 3D models, regardless of the format. Sections on calculating face and vertex normals, interpolation, and optimization

Figure 9.5 *A multi-part model being rendered using the tagging system to hold it together.*

can be found in the upcoming chapter. You will learn how to use each of these tips and tricks in a non format-specific way so that you can apply them to any model format, including your own.

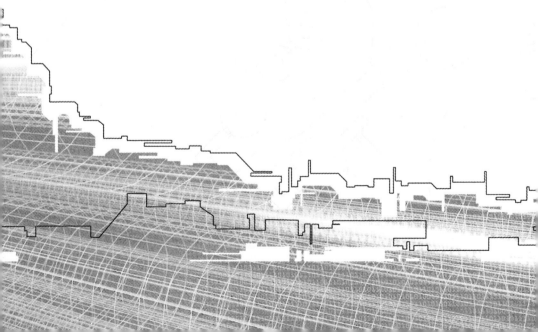

CHAPTER 10

TIPS, TRICKS, AND METHODS

T his chapter aims to give you a few good tips and tricks that you can apply to any 3D model that you come across. Using the methods here, you will be able to apply lighting to your models, move them around, and even optimize your rendering code a little bit. You first learn how to calculate face and vertex normals, which will enable you to apply lighting to your model. Face normals give you a flat-shaded model, whereas vertex normals give you a smooth-shaded model.

Calculating Face Normals

If you want to have lighting in your scene, it is essential to have at the very least a normal vector for each triangle. Failure to do this will cause certain parts of the model to be unlit, or lit in a peculiar way.

There really isn't anything to calculating a face normal. Follow these steps:

1. First, you need two vectors in the plane of the triangle. Because you have three points that lie within the plane (the vertices of the triangle), it is easy to create two vectors. Going back to algebra or geometry, you might remember that a vector can be found by taking the terminal point minus the initial point. The points of the triangle are these points. The first vertex of the triangle (Vertex0) can be considered the initial point for both vectors, the second and third vertices are the terminal points of the first and second vectors (Vector1 and Vector2) respectively. Therefore, Vector1 will be Vertex1 minus Vertex0, and Vector2 will be Vertex2 minus Vertex0.

2. A vector normal to the triangle points straight up at a 90-degree angle to the triangle's plane. Taking the cross product of the two vectors you just found will yield a single vector, orthogonal to the plane. It is important that you always take the cross product in the same order. The vector produced by crossing Vector1 with Vector2 (Vector1×Vector2) is not the same as the vector produced by crossing them the other way (Vector2×Vector1). The two operations will produce vectors pointing in opposite directions. If some of your faces appear to be lit incorrectly, make sure you are

computing your vectors and cross products correctly. However, if *all* of your faces are lit incorrectly, try crossing your vectors in the opposite order. The normals may be pointing into the model, rather than out of the model, as they should be.

3. Before you send this vector to the renderer, be sure to convert it to a unit vector. Remember that a unit vector must have a magnitude of one. To create a unit vector, you divide each individual component of the vector by the vector's original magnitude. This can be done manually, or you can use the Normalize function of the CVector3 class.

Take a look at this chapter's first demo, found on the CD in the Code/ Chapter10/Normals/ directory, for a demonstration of face normals.

Calculating Vertex Normals

The other type of normal is called the vertex normal. Now, instead of one normal for each polygon, one normal is used for every vertex.

Why use vertex normals instead of face normals? The answer is simple—using vertex normals gives you a much nicer looking model. Instead of each polygon being flat-shaded, the lighting is now interpolated between the vertices, giving a nice smooth shade.

Figures 10.1 and 10.2 compare the visual difference between vertex and face normals. Quite a difference, eh?

Calculating vertex normals is not difficult. The first thing to do is calculate all of the face normals. Then, for each vertex, you must determine which faces share that vertex. Once you find all of them, add up all of those faces' normals, and divide by the number of shared faces. This will give you a new unit vector, which is called the vertex normal.

```
//pseudocode to calculate vertex normals from face normals
for each vertex
    for each face
        if face contains vertex
            add the normal of the face to the normals of any
            other faces that share the vertex
    to obtain the final normal for the current vertex
    divide the vector calculated by adding all the face normals together by
    the number of faces sharing the vertex
```

Figure 10.1 *A flat-shaded model using only face-normals for lighting.*

Figure 10.2 *A smooth-shaded model using vertex normals.*

Creating Your Own Format

Creating your own 3D model format can be very beneficial to your game. By "rolling your own," you can include whatever data you need, from vertices to animations in whatever order and whatever form you want. You can also include other data such as textures or even game-specific data such as character dialogue. Best of all, you are not limited by the constraints of an existing format, and you can change the format to fit your needs as you go.

The first thing you must decide about your format is whether it will be stored in text or binary form. Both ways have advantages and disadvantages, discussed in the following sections.

Text-Based Format

If the format is stored in a text-based form, you sacrifice some storage space for readability. A text-based format will generally take up more room, due to each character using a full byte ("255" will take three bytes in text, only one in binary). Space may be a lower priority than, for instance, readability. Most text-based formats can be opened in a text editor and modifications can be made to the data without needing a full-fledged editor. This makes it easy to do simple things such as change the textures on the model or even tweak vertex positions.

Another downside to text-based models shows up when you go to load them. Text files can be a real pain to parse, particularly if small mistakes such as an extra space, or a blank line, are inserted at an odd place.

Binary-Based Format

A binary format can solve many of these problems, but at the expense of readability. A binary-based format is generally easier to parse because the size of each data type, such as a float or a short, is the same throughout the file. A floating-point binary value is always the same number of bytes, whereas in a text file, the same number could be any number of bytes, depending on the number of digits. Both text and binary will work; pick the one best suited for your needs.

Planning the File

The next thing you need to think over is what you want to include in your files. Here are a few questions you might ask yourself during this process:

- How will the vertices be stored? Will you have a simple X, Y, Z floating-point triple? Perhaps each vertex will be one byte with a floating-point scaling and translation value for each mesh, much like MD2 does.

- How will textures be handled? Will you simply store filenames within the model? You could embed the whole texture file into the model if you wanted, or even skip textures altogether and include only color and lighting data. Texture coordinates must be considered as well. Will you have only one set texture coordinate for each vertex, or will you need multiple sets for environment or light mapping?

- How are faces stored? Do you simply use triangles, or a combination of triangles and quads, or just quads? Another possibility is to store the model using *n-gons*, polygons with no set number of vertices, for each face. You can even get rid of polygons completely and store your model as a group of curved surfaces. If you choose to go with the triangles-only method, will the format be optimized for triangle strips and fans or just individual triangles?

- What else will the face information contain? Obviously it must contain indexes into the vertex array, but what about material information, texture coordinates, or normals? All these things can be stored with the faces as well.

- Will you use skeletal or keyframed animation? Or how about a combination of both? The animation adds a lot to a model. Skeletal animation is harder to implement (nearly impossible if you do not have a formal editor, or are not converting from another format). For some applications you might not need any animation, preferring to store only vertices, faces, and material information.

- Will the model be singular or multi-part? Some formats like MD2 consist of only one mesh that defines the whole file, whereas other formats such as 3ds can contain multiple connected meshes. You can even define attachment points to connect other models like md3 does.

- Planning on using extra "goodies"? Some model formats include advanced features such as normal maps, bump maps, or curved surfaces. These are unique structures and must be stored in a separate part of the file.

- Will you be including extra information not directly affecting the model? Examples of this would be development information, copyright tags, and other game-related content such as character dialogue or AI information. Just because it's a model file does not mean you can't add whatever extra data you want. However, you will need to be careful about adding just any information. Before you go ahead and add information to a model file, ask yourself, "is it really necessary to add this, or it just bloat?" Adding unneeded information to model files, or any type of file for that matter, will take up extra space. You may need to stop and reconsider adding information that has little or no effect on what the audience of your game will see or perceive. If you need to keep the overall size of your game to a minimum, take care to keep from blowing up the file size on your models by adding trivial or useless information. Those few extra bytes could probably be used more effectively in another part of the game.

- Do you plan on expanding your format later? The answer to this question could affect the design and layout of the format, even the way the format is stored. You can choose to make many assumptions about the model, such as the maximum number of vertices, or you can choose to make no assumptions at all. If you want a very expandable format, you might lay it out like the 3ds format does, with chunks and sub-chunks. This approach would allow you to add chunks later in the process without requiring you to rewrite all of your code. On the other hand, if your format will stay the same throughout the development process, you can use a more concrete layout. Keep in mind that a format that makes more assumptions trades expandability and modularity for ease of use and more efficient file I/O, whereas a format that makes no assumptions swings the other way.

- Last, will your models require any special treatment? For instance, if you want to stream models to gamers over the Internet or a network, you will need to take special considerations when designing and compressing your models in order to stream them as efficiently as possible. Other models may be required to be compatible with other parts of the game, such as scripts or shaders, that change the way they are displayed or control the way the models act or move. Be sure to check that out before designing your format. Nothing is worse than having to go back to the drawing table because you forgot to plan for one of these scenarios.

- Now you need to work out how data will be stored in the file. Will you have a header at the start? What will it contain? It helps to sit down with a pen and paper and draw a diagram of your file structure, an example of which is shown in Figure 10.3.

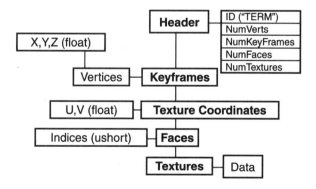

Figure 10.3 *An example file structure. This chart shows the layout for a new file format. It shows what is included in the file, as well as the order. The datatype of each section is also shown; the vertices are made up of floats and the indexes are unsigned shorts.*

Once you have that down exactly how you want it, it is time to create a way to make these new files.

Creating the Files

If your new format is very similar to an existing format, you can write a converter. A converter simply takes the data you want out of the original file and puts it into your new format, leaving behind anything you do not need, and adding any extra data such as normals or texture data.

If your format is slightly more bizarre, or too different from an existing format to easily write a converter, there is still an option before writing a complete editor. You can use an existing editor to export your new format. Many popular 3D editors offer packages that can be used to write your own import and export plug-ins. Some, such as 3D Studio Max, even have their own scripting language (MaxScript). Others have a software development kit that is used to write plug-ins. MilkShape 3D is an example of this. The MilkShape SDK is available free at the Chumbalum Soft site, as well as on the CD of this book.

Finally, if neither of these is an option, you can write your own editor, tailored specifically to your special format. Keep in mind that this can be a complicated, time-consuming process. I would definitely recommend checking out the other options before delving into writing your own editor.

The format I created in this section is similar to the MD2 format. However, I decided to leave out the optimization information, trim down the header, and embed texture data into the file.

This new format is now more suited to my application than MD2 was. Because I do not want people to be able to edit the skin on the model, I simply embedded the image file into the model file. Also, because I have no desire to use the optimization information included in the MD2s, I simply got rid of it. Because it no longer exists in the file, I removed all trace of it from the file's header as well. Because I added the image data to the file, I added a section of the header that will tell the program where to find this data as well.

I decided the easiest way to create my format would be to create an MD2 file and texture files first, and then write a converter to convert and combine them into one single file. Figure 10.4 shows the result.

If you look at the CD in the directory for this chapter (`/Code/Chapter10/`), you will see the converter I created, as well as some sample files and code to load this new format into your programs.

Figure 10.4 *The brand new, never seen before.TERM format in action.*

Linear Interpolation

Linear interpolation is the basis behind all keyframe animation. Although it has been discussed very briefly in previous chapters, this section looks at it more deeply in a general form.

Linear interpolation is one of the most useful game programming techniques. It is used to generate new frames in-between keyframes of traditional vertex-animated models. It can also be used to position an object between two end points, depending on the current time or other factors. If a monster is supposed to be at the end of a straight path after five seconds, you can use linear interpolation to determine where the monster should be at one second, two seconds, or any other time value. This allows you to move the monster along its path at a constant speed.

When you linearly interpolate between two points, you are finding a point on the line connecting the two. To find the desired point, you need three things—the ending point, the starting point, and an interpolation value. The interpolation value is a floating-point value between 0 and 1. If the interpolation value is 0, the result is the starting point; if it is 1, the result is the very end point; if it is somewhere in the middle, well, so is the result.

The general formula for doing this is as follows:

$$p_0 + (p_1 - p_0)t$$

Where P0 is the starting point, P1 is the ending point and t is the interpolation value.

Take a look at the example in Figure 10.5.

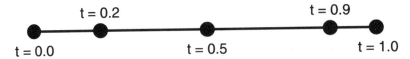

Figure 10.5 *Interpolating along a line. The object is at the beginning of the line when t = 0 and the end of the line when t = 1. When t is any other value, the object is in between the endpoints.*

The linear interpolation method most often used in games is called *linear interpolation with respect to time*. A time to get from point A to point B is provided, and at any given time, for instance every frame, the character or object must be drawn in the correct place. Linear interpolation is the lifesaver here. The only problem is calculating the current interpolation value.

First, you determine the amount of time that has elapsed since the object started moving. Then, to calculate the interpolation value, you take the elapsed time, divided by the total time the object should take to move the entire distance. For example, if 7.22 seconds have elapsed, and the object must reach the end in a total of 10.0 seconds, the interpolation value is 7.22/10.0 or 0.722. Be sure that your units on the elapsed time, and the total time are the same. If one is seconds, and the other is milliseconds for instance, the desired effect will not occur.

Take a look at Figure 10.6 for a picture of an object moving with respect to time.

This section also has a demo included on the CD; check it out in `/Code/Chapter10/Linear Interpolation/`!

Optimization Tips

Part of the fun in game development is squeezing out those last few frames per second and cramming as much information, graphics, and data into your game as possible, while still staying within acceptable limits for size and speed. Here, you will learn about a few optimization tips you can use along with your 3D models.

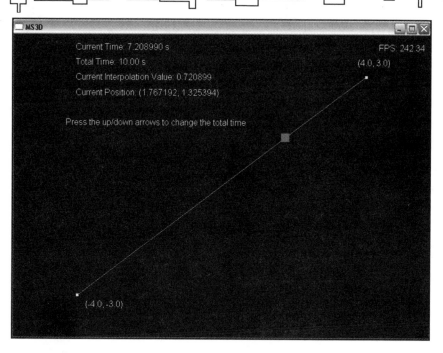

Figure 10.6   *An object moving with respect to time.*

- *Display Lists*: OpenGL contains a very useful feature known as display list. A display list holds compiled geometry. This is particularly good for static models because you only have to compile the list once and then you can display it many times. By using a display list, you can cut down the processing time tremendously. To use display lists in OpenGL, you should look into the following functions: `glGenLists`, `glNewList`, `glCallList`, and `glDeleteLists`.

- *Vertex Arrays*: Vertex arrays are another option for optimizing geometry. There are three types of vertex arrays in OpenGL. The first is simply an array holding the vertices in the order they need to be rendered. After setting the vertex array information using `glVertexPointer`, you can use `glDrawArrays` to render the data. The second type of array is an extension of the first. Using functions such as `glNormalPointer`, `glTexCoordPointer`, and `glColorPointer`, it is possible to add normal, texture coordinate, and color data into the arrays as well. The third type is an indexed array. An indexed array is the same as a standard array with one exception. Instead of just running through the array from beginning to end, an array of indexes into the array is used. The index array specifies the order in which the vertices, texture coordinates, colors, and normals are to be rendered. Using this approach, vertices can be reused, leading to a smaller array. The procedure is the same until you get to the glDrawArrays call. For an indexed array, glDrawArrays should be replaced with glDrawElements.

- *Compiled Vertex Arrays*: Although vertex arrays are fast, compiled vertex arrays are faster. Newer versions of OpenGL define an extension that allows you to compile your vertex arrays much like you compile a display list. The disadvantage here is that the data within the arrays cannot be modified without first unlocking the array, so compiled vertex arrays are best left to static objects. To use compiled vertex arrays, you should look into glLockArraysEXT and glUnLockArraysEXT as well as the functions for regular vertex arrays.

Conclusion

You now have a bag of tips and tricks that you can apply to almost any model format. You can calculate normals for models that do not include them within the file, enabling you to apply lighting to your 3D models and thus give them a more realistic look. You can also calculate where an object should be at a certain time using linear interpolation. This is especially useful when animating objects that use snapshots of the model to represent different positions. Using linear interpolation, you can create more snapshots to fill in the gaps between the originals and create a model that animates smoothly.

You also learned various techniques you can use to optimize your display and render code to increase the overall speed of your engine. This extra speed allows you to add more game-specific elements, or simply increase the frame rate when running the game.

Next up are the appendixes. In the appendixes, you will find a table that shows various file formats, along with the editors that create them. You will also find an introduction to STL vectors; useful if you need resizable arrays or if you need the special functions such as searching and sorting that STL vectors offer. You will also encounter a section that describes some of the paths that you may want to take in the future and suggests some Web sites and books for further reading.

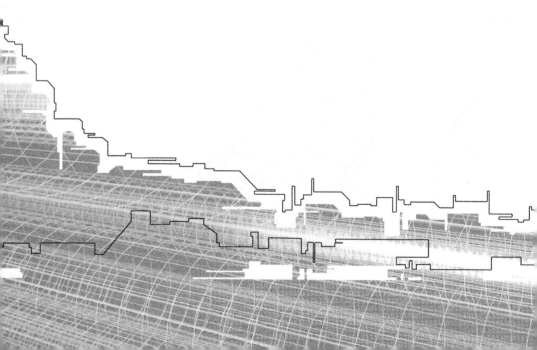

APPENDIX A

Common 3D Model Formats

Not sure what a particular model is used for? This handy chart lists some of the more common formats and which application, game, or editor they come from.

Table A-1   Common 3D Model Formats

Extension	Editor/Uses	Links
3DMF	3D Meta File, QuickDraw3D	http://www.apple.com
3DO	Jedi Knight	http://www.lucasarts.com
3DS	3D Studio Max: Binary-based format	http://www.discreet.com
ACT	Genesis 3D Engine	http://www.genesis3D.com
ASE	3D Studio Max: Essentially a text-based version of 3ds	http://www.discreet.com
ASC	3D Studio Max: Simple ASCII-based format containing only a minimum of data	http://www.discreet.com
B3D	Bryce 3D	http://www.corel.com
BDF	Okino	http://www.okino.com
BLEND	Blender	http://www.blender.nl
CAR	Carrara	http://www.eovia.com/carrara
COB	Calgari TrueSpace	http://www.calgari.com
DMO	Duke Nukem 3D	http://www.3drealms.com
DXF	Autodesk Autocad	http://www.autodesk.com

Table A-1   Common 3D Model Formats (continued)

Extension	Editor/Uses	Links
HRC	SoftImage 3D	http://www.softimage.com
INC	POV-Ray	http://www.povray.org
KF2	Max Payne animations and poses	http://www.maxpayne.com
KFS	Max Payne mesh and material information	http://www.maxpayne.com
LWLO	Lightwave layered file object	http://www.newtek.com
LWO	Lightwave object file	http://www.newtek.com
LWS	Lightwave scene file	http://www.newtek.com
MA	Maya ASCII-based format	http://www.aliaswavefront.com
MB	Maya	http://www.aliaswavefront.com
MAX	3D Studio Max	http://www.discreet.com
MD2	id Software's Quake II	http://www.idsoftware.com
MD3	id Software's Quake III	http://www.idsoftware.com
MDL	id Software's Quake	http://www.idsoftware.com
MDL	Valve's Half-Life	http://www.valvesoftware.com
MDL	Serious Sam	http://www.croteam.com
MS3D	Milkshape 3D format	http://www.swissquake.ch/chumbalum-soft
OBJ	Alias|Wavefront	http://www.aliaswavefront.com
PSK	Unreal/Unreal Tournament Mes	http://www.unrealtournament.com/
PZ3	Poser	http://www.curioslabs.com
RAW	Raw Triangles	(None)

Table A-1 Common 3D Model Formats (continued)

Extension	Editor/Uses	Links
RDS	Ray Dream Studio	http://www.metacreations.com
RIB	Renderman File	http://www.renderman.com
SCN	Calgari TrueSpace	http://www.calgari.com
SKD	Max Payne skin data file	http://www.croteam.com
SKN	The Sims	http://thesims.ea.com
SLP	Pro/Engineer	http://www.ptc.com
STL	Stereo-Lithography Format	http://www.sdsc.edu/tmf/Stl-specs/stl.html
VRML	Virtual Reality Modeling Language	http://www.web3d.org
X	Microsoft's Direct X format	http://www.microsoft.com
XGL	Various CAD Programs	http://www.xglspec.com

APPENDIX B

STL VECTOR PRIMER

—By Sean Kent

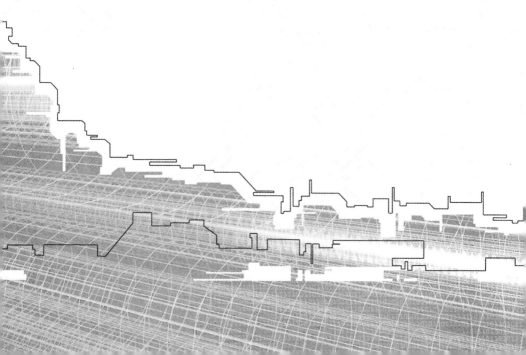

A s you have been reading through this book, you have no doubt heard plenty about the mathematical construct known as a *vector*. Well, here you are going to be introduced to another kind of vector, a *data storage vector*.

The Standard Template Library (STL) is a collection of container classes, iterator classes, and other utility classes and functions. A container is just that, it contains data of a user-specified type. The nice thing about STL containers is that they clean up after themselves, meaning that any memory they allocate, they also free. However, this doesn't include any memory you allocated. Iterators are a type of class that points to the data contained within a container class. An iterator has the capability to move through the elements inside of the container, giving you access to the elements that the iterator points to.

The STL Vector

The STL vector class (from now on just called a vector) is a container object that stores its elements in a linear arrangement, allowing for fast insertions and deletions at the end of the vector, and slower insertions and deletions in the middle or at the beginning.

When using the function vector<>::end, the return value will be the element after the last element in the vector. You will find that this "past the end" theme is repeated throughout STL.

The Basics of Using Vectors

The first thing you need to do to use a vector is to include the header file that it is contained in:

```
#include <vector>
```

You will notice that there is no .h extension on it, which is not a typo. STL headers in all of the implementations that I have used do not

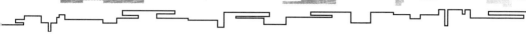

have an extension. The next thing you need to do is to declare a vector; in this case, you are declaring a vector of integers:

```
std::vector<int> vec; // Declares a vector that will contain integers.
```

So what is up with this std:: thing? Well, std is a namespace, which I won't go into much, other than to say that for a C++ program, all you need to do to avoid using this std:: is to add this line after the include:

```
using namespace std;
```

However, in a C++ program where you have multiple files, including headers and such, it is generally a good idea to just stick to using the std:: extension to prevent including namespaces unintentionally.

All right, so far you have included and declared a vector that will contain integers. Now you will insert some data into it. Inserting data at the end of a vector is easy; you just use the push_back function. The following code will insert the numbers 0–9 at the end of the vector:

```
for(int i=0; i < 10; i++)
vec.push_back(i); // Inserts i onto the end of the vector
```

To remove data from the end of a vector, you simply use the pop_back function. The pop_back function takes no arguments, and returns void. So, if you wanted to remove that last nine from the vector, you would do the following:

```
vec.pop_back(); // Removes the 9 from the end of the vector
```

Now that you have some data stored in your vector, you need to learn how to access the data. To do so, you use a little thing called an iterator. An iterator at its most basic form is just a class that gives you access to the data stored in a container on an element-by-element basis. You can use iterators for inserting, deleting, searching, and sorting the data stored within said container. So let's create an iterator in order to walk through your data and print it:

```
std::vector<int>::iterator l, endi;
endi = vec.end(); // Returns the element "Past the end" of the
// last element
for(l = vec.begin(); // Returns the first element in the vector
     l != endi; // Checks to make sure that we are not at the end
       ++l) // Moves l to the next element, using ++l instead of l++ is
// faster because you don't create a copy
```

```
{
    cout<<"Vector vec contains [ "
    <<*1 // the * operator returns a reference to the element 1 points to
    <<endl;
}
```

Not that difficult, eh? To insert data into a vector at any point, you must use the vector<>::insert() function. A warning, though: If you find that you are doing a lot of insertions and deletions anywhere except at the end of a vector, it is advisable that you look into one of the other container classes instead. Insertions at points other than the end of a vector are more expensive than at the end. To insert at, say, the beginning of a vector, you must first obtain an iterator pointing to the beginning, and then you merely call the insert function with the iterator, as well as the data you want to insert.

```
std::vector<int>::iterator 1 = vec.end();
while(1 != vec.begin())
{
    --1;
    vec.insert(vec.begin(), *1) // Insert at the beginning
                                // the element contained in 1
}
```

There are two ways to remove data from a vector at points other than the end. One is to use the vector<>::erase function and the other is to use the remove functions. The difference between them is that erase will remove and resize the vector, whereas remove will preserve the relative placements of the elements, but will remove the specified elements.

```
// Using remove:
std::vector<int>::iterator newend;
// Searches the vector for all 7's and removes them
newend = std::remove ( vec.begin( ), vec.end( ), 7 );

cout << "Vector vec with value 7 removed is [ " ;
for ( 1 = vec.begin( ) ; 1 != vec.end( ) ; 1++ )
    cout << *1 << " ";
cout << "]." << endl;

// To change the sequence size, use erase
```

```
vec.erase (newend, vec.end( ) );

cout << "Vector vec resized with value 7 removed is [ " ;
for ( l  = vec.begin( ) ; Iterl != l.end( ) ; l++ )
    cout << *l << " ";
cout << "]." << endl;
```

The next section of code removes all occurrences of 7 and resizes the vector.

```
// Using just erase:
vec.erase(vec.begin(), vec.end(), 7);
```

The complete set of the remove functions includes remove_if, remove_copy, and remove_copy_if. The remove_copy and remove_copy_if functions create a new range of values, copying only those values that are not part of the value specified. The remove_copy_if and remove_if functions take a function argument called a binary predicate, which is a true-false function that will return true for those elements that match the predicate, and false for all others. These functions then remove all elements that meet the binary predicate.

```
bool gt6( int val )
{
    return (val > 6); //returns true if greater than 6
}
.
.
.
std::vector<int> v2;
newend = std::remove_copy_if ( vec.begin( ), vec.end( ),
v2.begin( ), gt6 ); // copies to a new vector containing all values
// less than or equal 6
```

Sorting

At some point, you will likely want to sort your vector so that you may do cool things like use a binary search to find elements. Sorting a vector is a fairly simple process; you just use the sort function. The sort functions are included using the algorithm header.

```
#include <algorithm>
.
```

```
// The following code will sort your vector of ints in ascending order
std::sort(vec.begin(), vec.end());
```

The sort algorithm can also take a function argument that will be used to determine whether an item should be moved. STL has several of these functions already; you just need to include the `<functional>` header.

```
#include <functional>
#include <algorithm>
.
.
.
//sorts using the greater function object ( descending order )
std::sort(vec.begin(), vec.end(), greater<int>());
```

The greater<int>() part is actually a function object, which is basically an overloaded operator() that's contained within a structure or a class.

Searching

There are a few methods for searching a vector; however, this section covers only the use of the find functions as well as the binary search functions. The find functions work on both sorted and unsorted vectors. They work by comparing every element to the value being searched for. The binary search functions require a sorted vector, but they take significantly less time to find the element.

The find function has four versions. They are find, find_end, find_first_of, and find_if. The find function finds the first occurrence of an element. The find_if function finds the first occurrence of an element that meets a specified condition. The other two functions, find_end and find_first_of, aren't covered here.

To use find, simply call it with the range you want to search and the element you want to find. So, to find a number within a vector of integers, you would do the following:

```
#include <algorithm>
.
.
.
```

```
// Starts at the beginning of the vector, and proceeds to the end
// Till it finds a 7, or returns the element past the end if it doesn't
std::vector<int>::iterator i;
i = find(vec.begin(), vec.end(), 7);
if(i != vec.end()) // We found it
    .
    .
    .
```

To use the find_if function, you simply do the following:

```
#include <algorithm>
    .
    .
    .
bool IsGreaterThan5( int val )
{
    return (val > 5);
}
    .
    .
    .
std::vector<int>::iterator i;
//Will find the first element that is greater than five
i = find_if(vec.begin(), vec.end(), IsGreaterThan5);
if(i != vec.end()) // if we found it
    .
    . // Do stuff
    .
```

The binary search functions require a sorted vector, but can take significantly less time to find the element you are searching for. The binary search functions are binary_search, lower_bound, upper_bound, and equal_range. The binary_search function returns true if the element searched for exists. The lower_bound function finds the first occurrence of an element within a vector, or the position it would be at if it existed. The upper_bound function finds the element past the last occurrence of the element searched for within a vector, or where it would be if the element searched for existed. The equal_range function is just a combination of the lower_bound and upper_bound functions.

To use the binary search functions, you simply pass it the range of sorted elements you want to search and the element you want to find.

```
#include <algorithm>
.
.
.
std::vector<int> vec;
for(int j = 0; j < 10; j++)
{
    vec.push_back(j); // Insert 2 copies of the number at the end.
    vec.push_back(j);
}
sort(vec.begin(), vec.end()); // Sort the vector
bool found = binary_search(vec.begin(), vec.end(), 7); //Is there a 7?
assert(found == true); //should be
std::vector<int>::iterator k, l;
k = lower_bound(vec.begin(), vec.end(), 5); // Find the first five
l = upper_bound(vec.begin(), vec.end(), 5); // Find the item past the five
assert(*k == 5); // should be the first five
assert(*l == 6); // Should equal the element after the last five
```

Using Your Own Objects

So far, you have just been using vectors containing integers. Although integers are fine and dandy, you will probably want to use your own user-defined types with vectors. This section covers a few issues about using your own objects with vectors.

The first thing you need to do before you can store an object in a vector is define that object. An object that is going to be stored in a vector should include a copy constructor, because copy constructors are used when moving objects around. An overloaded assignment operator can also be helpful.

```
class MyObject {
    int age
int height; //in CM
public:
    MyObject() {}
    MyObject( int a, int h ) : age(a), height(h) {}
```

```
    // Copy Constructor
MyObject(const MyObject& a) : age(a.age), height(a.height) {}
    void SetAge(int a) { age = a; }
    void SetHeight(int a) { height = a; }
    int GetAge() { return age; }
    int GetHeight() { return height; }
    //Overloaded assignment operator
    MyObject& operator=(const MyObject& r) {
age = r.age; height = r.height; return *this; }

};
```

There is the basic object. To tell a vector to use it, you simply replace the int portion of the vector with MyObject:

```
std::vector<MyObject> vec; //vector to hold MyObject types
```

Now comes the tricky part—storing a MyObject inside of the vector. To do so, you call push_back with a MyObject, like so:

```
.

.

.
// Stick 10 random MyObject's into the vector
for(int j = 0; j < 10; j++)
{
    vec.push_back(MyObject(rand()%20+1, rand()%120 + 1));
}
```

To sort the objects, you must either overload the < operator or supply the sort function with another function. You will notice in the example code that you are passing everything by reference. This avoids a copy and thus saves you memory and time. This example sorts the vector by age:

```
#include <algorithm>
.

.

.
bool LesserAge( MyObject& l, MyObject &r)
{
    return (l.GetAge() < r.GetAge());
}
//or:
```

```
bool operator<( MyObject& l, MyObject &r)
{
    return (l.GetAge() < r.GetAge());
}
    .
    .
    .
sort(vec.begin(), vec.end(), LesserAge); // Sorts by age
sort(vec.begin(), vec.end()); // Sorts by age using <
```

Because the find function uses the == operator, you must overload it to work with your class. This is a simple operation:

```
#include <algorithm>
    .
    .
    .

bool operator==(MyObject l, MyObject r)
{
    if(l.GetAge() != r.GetAge())
        return false;
    if(l.GetHeight() != r.GetHeight())
        return false;
    return true;
}
    .
    .
    .
std::vector<MyObject>::iterator j;
j = std::find(vec.begin(), vec.end(), MyObject(10, 120));
if(j != vec.end()) //We found it
    .
    .
    .
```

The equality operator (== operator) is used in comparisons to determine whether one element equals another. However, it will only work on C++ defined types. To get around this limitation, you can overload it to accept other types. In this case, it is overloaded to accept MyObject types and to compare them based on both age and height. However,

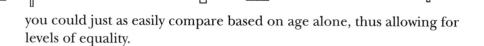

you could just as easily compare based on age alone, thus allowing for levels of equality.

Pointers

One of the disadvantages of storing an object inside of a vector is that whenever it gets moved, it has to copy the entire object to its new location. For small vectors, this may be possible, but when you start to get larger vectors, it becomes unacceptable. The way to avoid this is to use pointers. A pointer is quite a bit smaller than most objects, so moving them around takes a lot less time. However, because pointers use memory you have allocated, you must also remember to free that memory when you are done.

Declaring a vector to hold pointers to objects is fairly simple; you just replace the MyObject portion with the appropriate conversion:

```
std::vector<MyObject*> vec;
```

To put something into the vector, all you really have to do, from the last code, is add the new operator:

```
.
.
.
// Stick 10 random MyObject's into the vector
for(int j = 0; j < 10; j++)
{
    vec.push_back( new MyObject(rand()%20+1, rand()%120 + 1));
}
```

Sorting the vector is a bit different, because the sort operator will use a binary predicate that you specify or the < operator by default. Because a pointer is just an integer, the < operator will sort by the memory address and not the contents of the MyObject.

```
#include <algorithm>
.
.
.
bool GreaterAgePtr( MyObject* l, MyObject *r)
{
    return (l->GetAge() > r->GetAge());
```

```
}
.
.
.
sort(vec.begin(), vec.end(), GreaterAgePtr); // Sorts by age
sort(vec.begin(), vec.end()); // Sorts by age using < (memory address)
```

Searching has the same problem as sorting because it uses the ==
operator, except in this case there is a way around it:

```
#include <algorithm>
.
.
.
bool operator==(MyObject *l, MyObject r)
{
    if(l->GetAge() != r.GetAge())
        return false;
    if(l->GetHeight() != r.GetHeight())
        return false;
    return true;
}
.
.
.
std::vector<MyObject>::iterator j;
j = std::find(vec.begin(), vec.end(), MyObject(10, 120));
if(j != vec.end()) //We found it
.
.
.
```

Again, you are overloading the equality operator (==) just as you did
earlier. However, this time, it can compare a pointer to a MyObject
object and compare a MyObject object to itself. After you are done with
your vector of pointers, you must free the memory that you allocated.
This is a fairly simple process:

```
#include<algorithm>
.
.
.
```

```
template<typename T>
class DeletePtr
{
public:
    void operator()(T *elem)
    {
        delete elem;
    }
};
.
.
.
std::for_each(vec.begin(), vec.end(), DeletePtr<MyObject>());
```

The class `DeletePtr` with the member function `operator ()` is called a function object. All it does is delete `MyObject` pointers. If you wanted to, you could make it delete integer pointers by simply changing this line:

```
for_each(vec.begin(), vec.end(), DeletePtr<MyObject>());
```

to:

```
for_each(vec.begin(), vec.end(), DeletePtr<int>());
```

Simple and easy (and useful too).

Conclusion

If you are wondering about some of the applications of vectors in games, I have an idea. My idea is for a simple scene-graph. If you derive all of your objects from some base object, you could use a vector of pointers to the base object. This would allow you to easily do up-dates, collisions, and rendering. Because you would know that all objects before the current object had already moved and had been collision tested, you wouldn't have to test against them for your current object. Also, you could reuse vector elements, such as when a creature dies, so you set its vector element to an empty object, and when you need a new object, just reuse the empty ones.

Finally I would recommend that you do some more research into template programming, especially pertaining to the Standard Template Library. It has many types of containers, including deques, lists, sets, multisets, and maps. Each container has its own advantages and disadvantages, so picking the right one is not always easy. There is generally one container that will be better suited for a certain application than another.

APPENDIX C

GOING ABOVE AND BEYOND

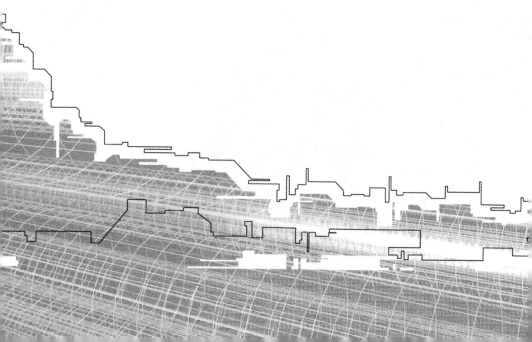

W ell, you made it. By now you should have a greater understanding of one of the most important parts in a 3D game, the 3D model.

Using the information in this book, you can now load, display, and animate several different types. No longer will you be stuck with a substandard model format or even be stuck coding in vertices and texture coordinates by hand!

Now that you know how to use these 3D models, you can recruit artists to begin making the content for your new game, freeing you to work on the programming aspects. You can fix those weird intermittent crashes every game seems to have, or maybe you can work on some cool new features to blow your audience out of their seat.

Even if you want to use a format that is not covered in this book, the information that you have just learned about will still prove valuable. The basic parts of a 3D model file—vertices, texture coordinates, and bones or keyframes—are found in nearly every format. All you need to do is search around for a format spec sheet to find out how the file is organized and set to work.

Good starting places to find papers detailing different formats include Wotsit's Format (http://wotsit.org), the Graphics File Format Page (3Dhttp://www.dcs.ed.ac.uk/home/mxr/gfx/3d-hi.html), and the "For Programmers" section of ziron.com (http://www.ziron.com/links/forprog.htm). Other good places to start looking include the Web site of the manufacturer of the accompanying program, and even your favorite search engine such as Google (http://www.google.com).

Best of all, you can use your new-found skills to develop a file format that fits your needs exactly. Never again be stuck wishing that your format supported embedded textures, or that it used skeletal animation instead of keyframes; now you can design your own file type, with just what you need.

This book is by no means the limit of your 3D adventures. New 3D model innovations are popping up each day, making games more realistic and more fun to play. Start taking a closer look at your favorite games; chances are you will see something that makes you say, "I wish my game could do that." Now, starting with the knowledge you have gained from this book, you can make it happen. Using the basic principles of skeletal animation, you can create realistic "ragdoll" systems. Ragdoll characters and other models move more realistically around the environment than traditional. From players sliding down hills, to the dead bodies of your defeated foes tumbling end over end into the bottomless pit, your ragdoll system can generate an unlimited supply of realistic animations on the fly. All without requiring any special animations or efforts from your poor, overworked, underpaid, stressed out artists.

Are your artists too busy to create variations for each animation such as walking or jumping? Perhaps you need many animations that are very similar to each other? Sounds like its time for a procedural animation system. A procedural animation system will allow you to vary animations on the fly. Your characters can finally reach toward different spots on a table, without requiring your artists to create a different animation for every reach; instead, the artist creates a generic animation. This animation is then modified by your program to go in the direction, or perform the exact move you want. Another application of a procedural animation system is to create more realistic and varied animations to break the monotony seen in most games. Everyone knows that a real person does not always walk at exactly the same speed in exactly the same way, so why should game characters? Using a procedural animation system, you can modify the speed, and even the appearance of the walk slightly to give it some variation.

Although these applications may seem subtle, they can greatly enhance a gamer's experience.

This is only the tip of the iceberg. There are many other cool and useful things you can do with your models and their associated code, even without enlisting the help of a talented artist. The sky's the limit.

One last thing before you run off to start work on your new game. Don't forget to check out the book's Web site at http://books.codershq.com. Here you can find additional supplemental code, errata, even spec sheets and code for loading model formats not discussed here. Also available on the site are ways to contact people if you get stuck, or need help flushing out that elusive bug in your code as well as links to papers and information that can help you create some of the extra things talked about briefly in this ending chapter.

There are even links to free 3D models and data that you can use in your games and programs.

Okay, let's get cracking, the game world is waiting for your new innovations, have fun.

For More Information

If you want to go above and beyond the call of duty and implement features beyond what is detailed here, there are a few sites you should check out as well as a few books to look into. First the links:

- `http://www.opengl.com`: At this official site, you can find out anything that deals with OpenGL. From a detailed description of each and every function, to news on OpenGL related topics, to updated drivers and information on new versions of OpenGL, this site contains it all.

- `http://nehe.gamedev.net`: The place to go to learn the basics of OpenGL. Jeff (NeHe) Molofee has created a wonderful site filled with tutorials, demos, and news pertaining to OpenGL. Many new programmers cut their teeth on OpenGL programming at this very site.

- `http://developer.nvidia.com`: At nVidia's developer's site, you can find information to help you optimize your 3D model rendering and other graphics code. At this site, you can find white papers on everything from new API features, to special effects, to card specific optimizations. Definitely a site every graphics programmer should visit regularly.

- `http://www.ati.com/developer/index.html`: Like nVidia, ATI also has a section of their site tailored to developers. Here you can find information related to the ATI card and its features, as well as how to use it within your programs.

- `http://www.gamedev.net`: One of the premier game development sites on the Internet. Gamedev.net contains many articles and references for programmers of all skill levels. The forums at Gamedev.net are also very active and are full of knowledgeable people who can help you out if you come across a problem you cannot solve.

- `http://www.flipcode.com`: Another great game development site, Flipcode caters more to the intermediate and advanced crowd.

Also with a myriad of tutorial and articles, as well as a fairly active forum, Flipcode should definitely have a space in your bookmarks.

- http://www.gamasutra.com: This site contains many types of articles, from technical articles on very specific subjects to game post-mortems that detail what went right and wrong within the development process of a certain game. This is another must-visit site for intermediate and advanced game developers.

- http://www.gametutorials.com: Game tutorials is an excellent place to learn about specific topics in game development and programming in general. Although mostly aimed at the beginning game developer, there is something for nearly everyone. Tutorials are in the form of source code with very extensive comments to explain what is going on and how it works.

Here are my favorite books on the topic:

- *OpenGL Game Programming* (Premier Press, ISBN 0761533303): A good intro to OpenGL game programming created by some of the staff of Gamedev.net. If you need to brush up on your OpenGL skills, this is the book to get. It even creates a small engine and game that you can expand on.

- *OpenGL Programming Guide,* aka *The Red Book* (Addison-Wesley Publishing, ISBN: 0201604582). The Red Book is a must for any serious OpenGL programmer. It goes through the features of OpenGL in an easy-to-understand manner complete with example code and demos.

- *OpenGL Reference Manual,* aka *The Blue Book* (Addison-Wesley Publishing, ISBN: 0201657651). Another essential book for when you are dealing with OpenGL. *The OpenGL Reference Manual* contains everything there is to know about the standardized OpenGL library. This book is aimed more at the intermediate and advanced folks, rather than beginners.

- *Game Programming Gems Series* (Charles River Media). This excellent series of books is aimed at the advanced crowd. These books contain everything from language tips and tricks to articles on AI. They also contain many articles dealing with 3D models and worlds, including topics such as mesh optimization, cell shading, shadowing, and progressive meshes.

What's on the CD

The CD contains many programs that will help you as you build your next 3D game. First and foremost are the code and example demos that show you how to load and use every format in this book, as well as mini-demos showing off some of the concepts such as skeletal animation and linear interpolation. All of the code and demos that go with the text are found in the /Code/Chapter*X* directory, where *X* is the chapter number.

Next comes a tool that will make sure you can run all of these demos. glSetup is a tool that will ensure that your computer contains the correct OpenGL drivers for your specific video card. This program will make sure you have the latest drivers for your card, even if your card is a bit outdated by industry standards. glSetup can be found in the /Programs/glSetup directory on the CD.

In order to use 3D models, someone must create them, either you or another artist. To help you or your artist along various modeling programs, both shareware and freeware are included:

- MilkShape 3D is one of the most popular shareware 3D model-ers available. With its capability to import and export many game specific formats, MilkShape3D (http://www.milkshape3d.com) is a must-have for any independent game developer. Get a taste of it by installing the 30-day trial included on the CD, which can be found in the /Programs/MS3DTrial directory.

- Another useful modeler is GMax. GMax is a free version of Discreet's (http://www.discreet.com) popular 3D Studio Max modeling package that is specifically tailored to games. Many new games even ship directly with GMax and the needed plug-ins for the specific games. It is found in the /Programs/Gmax directory.

- Recently open-sourced, Blender (http://www.blender.nl) is a powerful and free modeling package that will export in several useful formats. It can be used to create amazing 3D models and scenes. The installer can be found in the /Programs/Blender directory and the source code can be found in the /Programs/Blender/Source directory.

- 3D Canvas (http://www.amabilis.com) is created and sold by Amabilis Software. 3D Canvas uses an intuitive drag-and-drop method for creating and editing models. There are several versions of 3D Canvas with prices starting at free. The free version is what you will find on the CD at /Programs/3DCanvas.

- Anim8or (http://www.anim8or.com) is another small 3D package. It can be used to create low-poly models for games and other applications. It is free and can be found in /Programs/Anim8or/ directory on the CD.

Sometimes you need to convert between different file formats in order to use specific models in your programs. Deep Exploration is the program you need here. Created by Right Hemisphere, Deep Exploration offers a drag-and-drop interface and can convert between many file formats, both 2D and 3D. Deep Exploration can be found in the /Programs/DeepExploration/ directory.

To make your models less boring, you need to create textures to put on them. PaintShop Pro (www.jasc.com) and the gimp (www.gimp.org) are two of the best programs for doing just that. The demo version of PaintShop Pro can be found in the /Programs/PSP/ directory and the full, free version of gimp is located in the /Programs/Gimp/ directory.

Because you learned about using *Half-Life* (http://www.valvesoftware.com) models in association with the MDL library released with the *Half-Life* SDK, it is only reasonable that you can find the rest of the *Half-Life* SDK on the CD. Using this SDK you can create your very own *Half-Life* modification and try to attract some of the thousands of players that fire up the game every day to play their favorite modifications. The /Extras/HLSDK/ is where you want to look for this.

Last, there's the DirectX SDK (http://www.microsoft.com). Although none of the demos included actually use DirectX, many game engines do. You may want to port some of the demos included here over to DirectX in order to use them in your own engines and games. To do so, you will need this SDK. It's a big file, so if you are stuck without broadband, grabbing the SDK from /Extras/DirectXSDK/ will save you a lot of download time.

Index

M

GAME DEVELOPMENT.
IT'S SERIOUS BUSINESS.

"Game programming is without a doubt the most intellectually challenging field of Computer Science in the world. However, we would be fooling ourselves if we said that we are 'serious' people! Writing (and reading) a game programming book should be an exciting adventure for both the author and the reader."

—André LaMothe,
Series Editor

Gamedev.net

The most comprehensive game development resource

The latest news in game development
The most active forums and chatrooms anywhere, with
insights and tips from experienced game developers
Links to thousands of additional game development resources
Thorough book and product reviews
Over 1000 game development articles!
Game design
Graphics
DirectX
OpenGL
AI
Art
Music
Physics
Source Code
Sound
Assembly
And More!

Gamedev.net

Focus On
3D Models

PREMIER PRESS

An accompanying
CD is enclosed
inside this book